Praise

I0040357

'This book tells the fascinating story of how Catherine and her team strive to create opportunities for entrepreneurs and create jobs. The well-written and highly enjoyable book reveals the author's dedication to transforming the South African economy and society, fighting climate change, and her strong personal commitment to improving the lives of disadvantaged women and men.'
— **Raul de Luzenberger**, Deputy Head of the EU Delegation to South Africa

'This is a beautiful book on impact in the SME sector and offers powerful tips for anyone in the industry.'
— **Ntando Maseko**, business mentor, author and entrepreneur; Founder, Megalife Coaching Academy

'This book is a succinct, well-paced and insightful journey through two decades of finding new ways of growing small businesses, by a true pioneer in the sector. It is engaging, honest and insightful, and I highly recommend it to anyone with an interest in the mechanics of helping entrepreneurs and business owners achieve new levels of success.'
— **Anton Ressel**, Strategic Head of SME Support, Fetola

THE
ART
OF
ACCELERATION

How to create BIG opportunities
for small business

CATHERINE WIJNBERG

R^ethink

First published in Great Britain in 2025
by Rethink Press (www.rethinkpress.com)

© Copyright Catherine Wijnberg

All rights reserved. No part of this publication may be reproduced, stored in or introduced into a retrieval system, or transmitted, in any form, or by any means (electronic, mechanical, photocopying, recording or otherwise) without the prior written permission of the publisher.

The right of Catherine Wijnberg to be identified as the author of this work has been asserted by her in accordance with the Copyright, Designs and Patents Act 1988.

This book is sold subject to the condition that it shall not, by way of trade or otherwise, be lent, resold, hired out, or otherwise circulated without the publisher's prior consent in any form of binding or cover other than that in which it is published and without a similar condition including this condition being imposed on the subsequent purchaser.

Cover image © Shutterstock | Blan-k

To the people who have believed in me and supported my vision to make the world a better place. Especially to the wonderful clients and partners that have invested in Fetola's work and walked alongside us as we build bigger and better solutions.

To those who have joined our team as partners, suppliers, staff and mentors, who all bring their A game to work, looking constantly for ways to help others to grow.

To all the heroes and heroines with the courage to start and grow businesses, without whom none of our work would be possible.

To my family, with its long line of strong, courageous women.

Contents

Foreword

In the vast landscape of entrepreneurship, where dreams are sown, challenges embraced, and successes harvested, few voices resonate with the clarity of Catherine Wijnberg. Catherine is not just an entrepreneur; she is a visionary, and an inspiration to those intent on building businesses that not only survive but thrive.

It is with immense pleasure and respect that I write this foreword to Catherine's remarkable new work, *The Art of Acceleration: How to create big opportunities for small business.*

As a past chair of Fetola's board I have witnessed firsthand the dedication and passion that Catherine brings to her work. Her ability to cultivate strategic partnerships, empower women, and drive tangible results stands out in a world grappling with complex economic, social and environmental challenges.

In these pages, Catherine shares some of her personal journey while distilling invaluable insights on how to build an ecosystem where small businesses and economies can flourish. The lessons she imparts are practical; they are forged in the fire of real-world experiences. From her early days as an agricultural economist to the heights of running a business growth sector, Catherine's journey motivates aspiring entrepreneurs, seasoned business leaders, and policymakers alike.

In the pages that follow, Catherine shares her wealth of experiences, which are marked by audacity, setbacks, triumphs, and an unwavering commitment to the transformative power of entrepreneurship.

Her own roots in entrepreneurship run deep, anchored by the wisdom passed down from her entrepreneurial father in Ndola, Zambia. From these beginnings, she embarked on a journey that took her across continents, studying agriculture in Scotland and Australia, and eventually finding her calling in the dynamic world of business. Her narrative is not one of a smooth ascent to success but rather a testament to the indomitable spirit required to weather storms and emerge stronger, something she openly shares with the entrepreneurs that join her business programmes.

Catherine's business, Fetola, is a testament to her commitment to transforming the South African economy through the growth of small businesses. Her vision goes beyond mere economic expansion; it encompasses the creation of opportunities for women, youth, and rural communities to shape self-empowered futures. With a resolute belief that one woman can make a difference, Catherine has indeed become that difference.

The Art of Acceleration is more than a guidebook; it is a roadmap to designing successful programmes that address key social and environmental challenges in order to build sustainable, circular and inclusive economies. Catherine's narrative invites readers to embrace the challenges, learn from setbacks, and forge ahead with determination. It is a call to action for individuals, businesses, and governments to collaborate in building ecosystems that foster entrepreneurship, create jobs, and contribute to a more equitable and prosperous world.

As you read this book, I hope Catherine's story will inspire and guide you in a collective pursuit of building a future where thriving small businesses become the heartbeat of resilient economies all over the world.

Cecilia Kinuthia Njenga
Director, Intergovernmental Support and
Collective Progress UNFCCC

Introduction

I started writing this book with the intention of sharing all the knowledge and experience I've gained as an entrepreneur and accelerator of entrepreneurs, with the hope of inspiring impact investors, policy makers and practitioners that work with small businesses to invest their time and resources wisely in supporting those businesses to succeed. I realised, though, that in my determination to share everything useful, I had created something more like a company manual than a book. The last thing I want to do is write something that is a chore to read!

This is therefore a rewrite. I have chosen to include some of my own stories, including anecdotes of my failures and weaknesses, as these provide the best opportunities to learn and grow. I haven't, though, told you everything I've learnt – that would result in a very long book. Rather, I have taken a selection of the ideas and insights I think you will find most interesting and useful in your own journey in helping people to start and grow successful businesses at scale.

I didn't set out in life to become any sort of business growth guru. As a child, I dreamt of being an explorer, an adventurer or maybe a wildlife photographer. I was born in the small town of Ndola, Zambia, to an entrepreneurial family. My father was the founder of a large construction company that specialised in building government schools, hospitals and airports in the very rural provinces of the country. He had a remarkable ability to manage these remote sites using local, usually unskilled labour – more than 1 000 staff members across multiple sites. He coped with no electricity, no phones, little or poor road infrastructure, and with only infrequent and often patchy, weather-dependent shortwave radio communication. In hindsight, his super skill was his ability to reliably deliver consistency, even under the primitive circumstances of the 1960s and 70s, long before computers or cell phones. His methods rested on checklists and the triplicate notebook. Each leaf of the book clearly recorded the expectations – what to do, when and how. One copy was for the foreman, one was for the site file, and a master copy remained in the book. Clear, simple and replicable.

Returning to Zambia long after my parents passed away, I met people whose entire lives – and that of their families – had been changed through the work of my parents. By building schools in remote parts of the country, my father made high school education accessible and released hundreds of young girls from forced, early marriages. My mother, meanwhile, had given women the sewing skills to sustain themselves and their families. This history must have stuck, emerging later in my life in my passion to make a difference.

My experience as an entrepreneur started with a small tomato farm on rented land not far from Lusaka. My fiancé at the time was an energetic young farmer with a big, bold ambition. He spotted a gap in the market when tomato prices were high, before the annual flush of produce from rainfed farmers created oversupply. Every day he would rise before dawn to load crates of tomatoes precariously high onto his old and battered truck and drive into Lusaka to sell them at the market. This little farm, carved out of bush by hand, yielded enough profit in one season to buy a brand-new pickup truck. It was an exciting time, and the business bug bit me hard. We went on to start other ventures, and I have since started and owned businesses in five different sectors and in three African countries. These rich experiences keep me close to the needs of others as I work to help them succeed.

Small businesses are rightly regarded as the drivers of growth, and as a solution for unemployment, which besets so many communities across the world. In

South Africa alone, the expectation is for small, micro and medium-sized enterprises (SMMEs) to generate up to 90% of new jobs in the next decade.[1] This presents both a huge opportunity and a great challenge. Without a thriving small business sector, the future looks very bleak. With one, it is possible to create a growing economy that generates inclusive wealth and much-needed jobs.

I never tire of working in this space, as business is an exciting, dynamic and continually evolving field. Every industry sector and business poses a unique set of challenges and opportunities. I hope my enthusiasm helps to foster yours as you read this book.

The book is written in two parts. In Part One I discuss the origin of the company Fetola, before walking through the different elements of the Fetola Growth Method, which underpins the small-business accelerators we implement.

Part Two describes the different accelerators, with case studies to showcase how these methods are applied in practice. The case studies include a selection of unique problems and challenges, as well as an entrepreneur case study, to bring everything to life.

Let's get started!

PART ONE
THE PRINCIPLES OF SMALL BUSINESS SUCCESS

The purpose of this Part One overview is to give you the context in which we work, before moving on to the important building blocks needed to achieve results. I will start by taking you to my own origins with Fetola, the company I formed in 2006.

Fetola is a well-established social enterprise, with over 100 staff and consultants, which creates economically viable solutions to solve tricky social and environmental problems through the successful growth of small businesses. We operate in South Africa, which, like many other countries with developing economies, has manifold underlying economic, social and environmental challenges. As a result, many entrepreneurs are motivated to make a positive difference in their communities, either indirectly, through the jobs they create; or directly, through the business solutions they provide.

It's also important to understand that, as we mostly work with entrepreneurs from disadvantaged backgrounds who cannot afford to pay for business development services, our accelerators are heavily subsidised by social impact investors and corporate, donor and philanthropic partners. These people seek ways to create a better future for all, whether through improvements to livelihoods, equality, wellbeing or climate change, or in creating a healthier planet.

The methods shared in the following chapters have been used to accelerate over 1 500 individual enterprises, more than 87% of whom are still in business many years after graduation – nine times the national average! Of these entrepreneurs, across a wide range of sectors, 53,3% are women, 60,2% are youth, and 98% are black South African (as defined in the BBBEE Act). The eight-year average performance of businesses under acceleration is 39,1% revenue growth and 23,1% jobs growth.

Collectively, these enterprises generate positive impact across all seventeen of the sustainable development goals and through reduction of environmental impacts such as climate change.[2]

Fetola's big vision is to foster an ecosystem where we can together improve a billion lives by 2030. Come on in!

1
Where It All Began

I started Fetola in 2006, whilst I was completing my MBA and working a full-time job. At that time I was greatly frustrated by the constraints of working as an employee, and I was harbouring a burning passion to do more and be more. It felt I was missing my true purpose in life, and I began to ask myself, *What can one woman do to make a difference?*

The answer came out of my past experience as an entrepreneur in a wide range of businesses, countries and industries. I spotted a gap in the market to use these skills to help people, especially women, to start and grow successful businesses. Having personally felt the liberating power of business, I understood that this would have generational impact on their families and the communities around the women I was helping. That became my mission.

There was something more than that, though. I had also experienced failure and divorce, the resulting painful loss of everything I owned, and the struggle of starting from zero as the sole breadwinner for three daughters. This experience spurred me to use my lessons to help others to start right and to build businesses that would stay in business.

That dream has become Fetola – a successful social enterprise that helps people start and build successful, sustainable businesses. This success is achieved repeatedly, business after business. We use documented systems and methods, professional growth teams, agile technology solutions, and catalytic investment solutions.

Whilst our methods have been honed in South Africa, it is my firm belief that they are applicable in all emerging countries – and ecosystems – where small-business success is a critical component of society's wellbeing.

South Africa arguably has the strongest economy in Africa, but underlying this are vast contrasts in wealth, making it one of the most unequal countries in the world.[3] Alongside this characteristic, South Africa has the second highest youth unemployment in the world – around 50,5% in 2023.[4]

It was against this backdrop that the South African National Development Plan of 2012 emphasised the small-business sector as an essential solution for inequality, poverty and unemployment, pegging 90% of new jobs to come from the SMME sector.[5]

This is a challenge – you could call it the Everest of Everests of challenges. Fetola's job is to help scale this Everest by building businesses that grow the economy, create inclusive wealth and generate those much-needed jobs. The small businesses we advise are the foundation for the rest of the economy as it attempts this difficult task.

Building a partnership

Our first client for business growth services was the Old Mutual Foundation. Old Mutual is one of South Africa's oldest institutions, listed on the international stock exchange, with its origins as a people's mutual fund. It is a much-loved company across South Africa.

The opportunity for our partnership arose when the then head of Old Mutual shared a frustration that, in spite of working hard and supporting many small enterprises and charities all across South Africa, the foundation continually struggled to build visible impact or gain acknowledgement for their work.

This got me thinking. I submitted a proposal with the goal of clustering all their disparate initiatives into one unique, clearly branded programme, through which they could:

- Gain economies of scale

- Build impact

- Achieve results significant enough to be visible to others

We also reworked the expectation of the donation-based support used by the non-profit sector, replacing it with an outcomes-based model, whereby Fetola charged per measurable outcome. Most importantly, we set a vision to go beyond Old Mutual's expectations by delivering more than they anticipated in enterprise performance and visible success, with the aim that better-than-projected results would inspire them to increase the size of the programme every year.

This first tentative proposal grew into the award-winning Old Mutual Legends Programme – their flagship initiative from 2007 to 2014. It was a rich learning ground for Fetola, and we owe a lot of our current lessons, methods and innovations to this first programme. In fact, many of the original principles of this book – whilst subsequently improved, polished and adjusted – started there.

Looking back, I feel so grateful to that team at the foundation. It takes courage to say yes to innovative new solutions, pushing the boundaries in a large, established organisation, and the Old Mutual Foundation was the first of many clients to do so. Today we remain surrounded by innovative partners who are business-minded and passionate about making a tangible, measurable impact.

Building a team

Fetola is all about helping others to reach their vision of success. Entrepreneurs put themselves and their future in our hands, and partners entrust us with their investments. We have been given the job of caring for the goose that lays the golden egg – it's our job to make sure she hatches them all, and that the newly hatched go on to lay more eggs.

This is a specialist task because small businesses are not simply small versions of big businesses. They are different in their energy and fragility. A broad range of skill sets and great courage are needed to start and grow small businesses successfully. As their support team, we need to have matching skills and a deep understanding of all that is needed for their journey.

To do this for multiple businesses, across a range of geographies and situations, requires a team of staff, mentors, trainers and specialists. Those need to be people with exceptional intellectual and emotional intelligence, an agile mindset, and a sensitivity and understanding of the rigours of business ownership. By keeping our support team agile, innovative and forward-thinking, we can support the same attitude within the small businesses we work with. To be really exceptional, an acceleration team also needs to be able to match the entrepreneur's gender, sector, growth phase and changing needs.

Building a model

Much has changed since we launched our first programme in 2007. Then the accepted model was to work one on one with businesses, providing face-to-face training and mentoring. This was largely restricted to the main city centres, where the trainers and mentors lived.

We broke that mould by focusing our energies away from urban centres and towards the outlying areas, where there were no support structures, yet the need for support was – and still is – greatest. Classroom-only training was replaced by remote learning support (the first rudiments of e-learning, introduced long before it became the norm) and remote mentoring support. This experience stood us well when Covid struck – we pivoted seamlessly to remote mentoring and introduced online support and peer-group webinars at a time when entrepreneurs needed a sense of calm encouragement.

These methods have been crystalised into the Fetola Growth Method, which covers all the components we need to achieve consistent high performance.

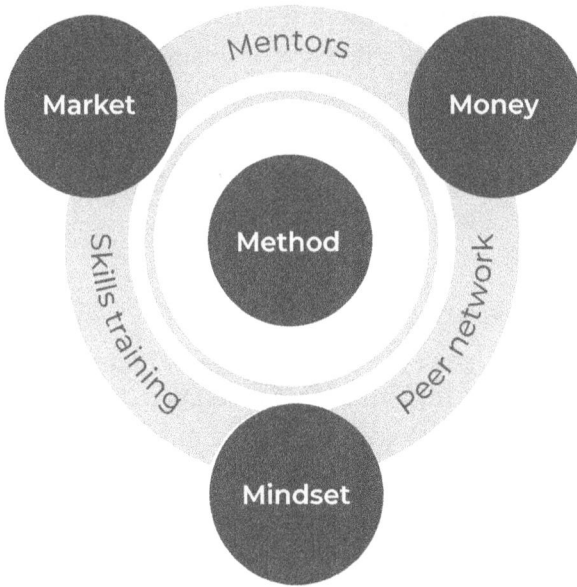

The Fetola Growth Method

Acceleration or incubation – a note on language

This book shares Fetola's bespoke model to help people start, grow and scale successful small businesses. The jury is out on whether this is incubation or acceleration.

As our methods are a blend of both, I have chosen to use the term 'acceleration', since this best describes Fetola's growth mindset and deliberate actions to avoid the dependency and resulting 'failure to launch' challenges that are common with pure incubation.

All the small businesses we work with operate within their own business premises. This means we are not limited to one specific type of business and gives us the freedom to work in any sector of our choosing. Our methods also encourage an empowering sense of independence for the businesses at all steps in their growth journey.

The acceleration team

This form of high-quality acceleration, in which the business is consciously supported to reach lasting success, requires much more than just a mentor. It requires a team of highly skilled individuals working in a coordinated and conscious manner, much like a Formula One racing team. At the time of writing, the team consists of 35 people in the Cape Town head office and another 60 mentors and specialists across the country.

Fetola accelerators operate on a hub and spoke model, with a team that is made of three parts:

1. **The programme management unit.** The standard structure is a project manager and senior project coordinator, supported by a senior lead

programme manager. This team manages the successful delivery of the multiple phases of the accelerator, ensuring individual performance is optimised and appropriate services are provided to each. They also manage entrepreneur relationships, formal reporting and client partnerships.

2. **The SMME services team.** These specialist teams deliver the individual components of the acceleration programme to each SMME. This includes portfolios consisting of mentorship, market readiness, training and investment readiness. These portfolios are responsible for delivering optimal solutions to individual needs, in order to maximise in-programme and long-term impact.

3. **The support team.** Core support services provide support to the project and portfolio teams through financial management, monitoring and evaluation, team upskilling, legal and governance, and partnership development.

Throughout this book, 'Accelerators' is used as a collective term for this team of accelerator programme staff, mentors, consultants and specialist providers that make up the growth solutions provided to the SMMEs.

Summary

I started my journey into business acceleration as a personal quest and challenge to myself. I'm amazed how this has grown to become a shared passion and purpose for so many.

The initial acceleration model was built on my personal experiences in starting, growing, and sometimes failing, in a wide range of businesses across five different sectors in three African countries. By constantly asking ourselves *What would the entrepreneur need?* and by recruiting highly skilled, entrepreneurial-minded people to the team, we have been able to build on our knowledge.

Chance often has a part to play in the life of an individual business, but to generate consistent results over many years – in different sectors and at various stages of growth – takes more than luck. Consistent success requires a willingness to listen and learn, and it needs a replicable method.

In the next chapters I'll take you through some of the individual components of the Fetola Growth Method that provide the foundation for this replicable success.

Key takeaways

To build a successful small-business accelerator, you need:

- Partners whose needs you can satisfy beyond their expectation

- A professional growth team that is passionate and skilled at helping entrepreneurs succeed

- Replicable methods and ways of working that ensure consistent results

- A proven, flexible model that can be adjusted to the specific needs of the sector and businesses under acceleration

- A driving purpose and passion for small business

2
Mindset

Our mindset is the sum of our opinions and attitudes. It encapsulates the way we think about ourselves, about others and about our circumstances. In a small business, where leadership plays a critical role, mindset relates to the attitudes and beliefs of the entrepreneur. After all, if I *am* my business, then how I think and feel directly impacts the fortunes of my business.

I'm passionate about mindset and its impact on one's ability to succeed as an individual and as a leader. It is the leader's personality, motivation, resilience and determination to succeed that make the business work or fail. Whilst there are many other factors, without the right leader – an entrepreneur with the right mindset – the business will not thrive. In helping people to start and grow successful businesses, our role is to find extraordinary individuals and to nurture them to their fullest potential.

The importance of leadership was one of the very first lessons we learnt in the business of small-business growth. In our first intake of the Old Mutual Legends Programme, we were given a mixed selection of candidates, ranging from large non-profit organisations to small rural cooperatives. We discovered a diversity of skill sets, languages, backgrounds and sectors. Our first intake included wood artists from deep rural Limpopo, a ceramic factory, a women's beading cooperative, a young ceramic artist and even a community group from the margins of a National Park. It was a very mixed bag and provided a rich learning experience.

Over the next two years, we invested energy and resources into a craft cooperative, helping them improve their retail space, understand and standardise their product costing and pricing, and improve their financial and business management processes. The business responded well on the programme, more than doubling its turnover, and we were delighted with the results. When we returned a year later, I was shocked (and embarrassed) to see that revenue had dropped and things were pretty much where they had been at the beginning. The dynamic energy was gone, the shelves were dusty, and product displays were uninspiring. It was almost as though we had never been there.

When I mentioned my frustration to their supervisor, she replied, 'Oh, yes – this always happens. They have been helped many times!'

This raw feedback got me thinking. As I looked deeper, I began to realise we had failed to truly understand the vision and purpose of the cooperative. Our outside 'growth lens' was seeking ways to fix the business and catapult their growth by increasing sales.

What we missed was that for the people running the cooperative, it was a 'home' – a community place of work, whereby they gained social standing and a sense of camaraderie and meaning. They earned sufficient for their needs and didn't align with our goal for greater financial success. In hindsight, we had completely missed the community's pervading belief system, in which the concept of wealth was a negative and alienating experience. Our interventions had neither understood nor addressed the underlying expectations and motivation of the cooperative's leadership.

The awareness of this failure led quickly to a change in method, out of which we embedded two fundamental principles in our work:

1. To take great care in selecting the entrepreneurs and business leaders we work with, to ensure our growth intentions are aligned

2. To follow a clear process, before we start, in understanding the vision of the leadership and purpose of the enterprise

Entrepreneur profiles

Effective marketing of a high-value accelerator programme will mean that you attract hundreds – maybe even thousands – of candidates. This will require you to sift through the candidates to find those that best meet the programme's expectations.

Our accelerators became known for their high value and results. They were oversubscribed by as much as 10 000, with ratios of 100:1 not uncommon. This ratio might be good for the ego and confirmation that our work is valued. If, though, the starting point of success is to identify individuals who are genuinely capable of growing a business, we must know which processes are best to select the one-in-a-hundred candidate.

Entrepreneurship is an unusual skill that requires, among many other factors:

- Strength of character

- Commitment to see things through

- Willingness to make tough, unpopular decisions

These are the characteristics of people who are different and who, interestingly, often feel like misfits in their own society, especially if they are the first entrepreneur in their family or community. Understanding and recognising what it means and how it feels to be an entrepreneur is critical in building an acceleration programme.

There is also a difference between an entrepreneur and someone with the potential to grow a business to scale. In layman's terms, I often describe the entry-level entrepreneur as a hustler, a jack of all trades, a dynamo, a rule breaker, a maverick. This bold, action-orientated personality is perfect for getting a business started. They jump in and just do it, using their drive and inner passion to overcome challenges, and a positive mindset to push through to success. This type of high-scoring entrepreneur loves to be hands-on at the centre of everything, solving problems and keeping many balls in the air.

To take the start-up to scale, though, demands another quality. It requires someone with both an entrepreneurial spirit and the ability to step up to the next phase of growth, handling the often repetitive and mundane tasks of the business. Those include managing staff, systems, finances, governance, compliance and quality. For the transition from start-up to business, the founder needs to let go and delegate. They need to step away from the role of first violin or solo guitarist and become the conductor of the orchestra.

When selecting your entrepreneurs, it's vital to understand your end goal. Are you looking to build many small businesses, or are you seeking to accelerate a single business idea to scale? Your answer will determine the type of leadership personality you are seeking.

A word of caution here: entrepreneurs reach out to accelerator programmes because they have a problem. Their businesses are either failing, or they are failing to grow as they would like. High-quality entrepreneurs recognise that success does not happen without effort and that quick fixes have limited longevity. Your job is to find out what the problem is. Is it something you can fix, and is the entrepreneur willing to take the required medicine?

What you select to work with is what you will have to work with, so choose wisely!

What entrepreneurs want

The South African context continues to change very fast. As small business is seen as the panacea to our many ills, more and more acceleration and incubation initiatives are being launched, creating a confusion of opportunities for entrepreneurs. Not only are entrepreneurs unsure which accelerator programme to join, but so too are investors. Whilst there are good opportunities out there, many are simply too good to be true, as the entrepreneur and investor will discover down the line.

Knowing how and where to fit your acceleration pro-gramme to the needs of your candidate means that you must put yourself in their shoes. Ask yourself:

- What goals would you be seeking?
- What outcomes would you be yearning for?
- What would you be prepared to do to achieve success?

Entrepreneurs are governors of their own worlds. They are in business for themselves because they value their freedom. They are by their nature independent self-starters. They want to reach their version of success, not yours. Crafting a marketing message that appeals to the right entrepreneur therefore requires constant self-reflection. Making sure the message reaches the right target audience – through personal networks, recommendations, social media and advertising – is an art. My guidelines are:

- Be authentic
- Talk in direct, simple language
- Get and keep a reputation for under-promising and over-delivering

Selection

Any racing pundit will tell you that picking winners is neither simple nor easy, yet a sound methodology, based on research and data insights, significantly increases the likelihood of success.

To increase your chances of success, you will need to consider four key selection attributes. As illustrated in the figure below, these are:

1. The entrepreneur or leadership profile

2. The business model

3. The size of capital investment needed to succeed

4. The market potential for the products and services

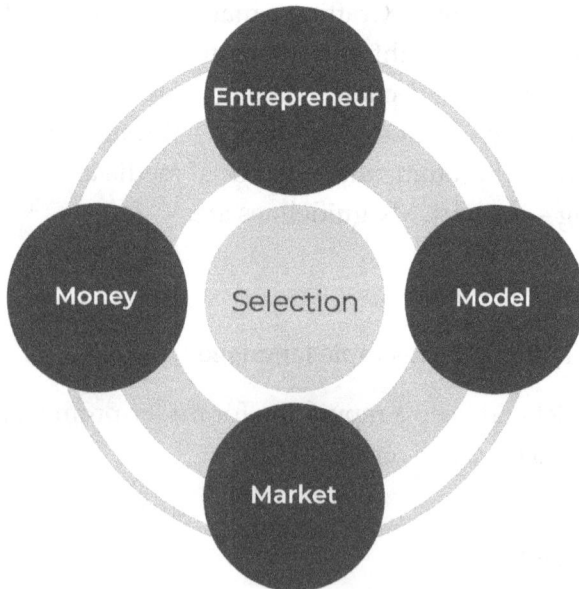

Key selection attributes

It stands to reason that the greater the investment you are risking, the more detailed and intense the due diligence in selection needs to be. For example, you don't need to triage who can sign up for a low-cost initiative such as online training; but where large sums of money will be invested in a business, selection governs your likely return on investment.

A single online test for selection would be ideal, but this is not yet possible. We use profiling as just one of a pipeline of selection tools, and as we work closely with psychometric specialists and use AI to refine and improve these methods, we are becoming more confident in the results.

It's easier to select established businesses whose history, track record and tangible evidence of performance help in the decision making. Even then, though, it's good to have a 'boots on the ground' approach, allowing you to eyeball the business before investing your time and money. We learnt the importance of this at Fetola when, in the early days, after investing significant funds in an in-person seven-day training camp, we discovered that one of the businesses simply didn't exist. On another occasion, a candidate claimed to have a learning lab and sent us pictures of a room full of computers. The subsequent site visit revealed he had hired some computers for the photoshoot to give the impression of a going concern. Full marks for creativity and the 'fake it till you make it' ethos, but a fail on ethics and authenticity!

Experiences like these keep us alert to misinformation and reinforce the need for checks and balances, such as site visits, to uncover them.

Building leadership mindset

Assuming we have a selection of the best entrepreneurs in town, where to from here?

The ideal mindset in a leader is one of calm self-confidence and a clear purpose. Good leaders are enthusiastic and positive, and they have high energy for the journey to success. They are resilient and able to bounce back from the inevitable stumbles on the road to success. They are eager to learn and have an open, inquisitive mind. On the flip side, they are willing to acknowledge their failures and flexible enough to let go of fixed ideas.

Those who create a balanced pathway, unfazed by either disaster or great success, are most likely to succeed in the long term. Our job is to help them achieve this.

There are many excellent tools that support personal growth. One of them is the Positive Intelligence course by Shirzad Chamine, which has a nifty app and offers daily podcasts designed to help uncover *What holds me back?*[6]

Another personal transformation tool, which has stuck with me for more than a decade, is the exercises outlined in *The Breakthrough Experience* by Dr John Demartini.[7] These examine life in seven segments, asking the questions *What is really important to me?* and *How will I achieve these goals?* My personal experience, when using the method for the first time, was of wonder at the concept of life through a new, holistic lens. I was able to identify my own deep, personal inner purpose. The exercises helped align my personal passion and purpose with my business purpose, and they unlocked the energy, enthusiasm and commitment I needed to succeed. I see a similar reaction from the entrepreneurs we take through the exercises – a powerful awakening within, and the starting point of personal transformation towards their individual and business success.

When we falter, it's often because our personal target has slipped out of view. That might be because we didn't have a clear picture in the first place, or because the business has moved on, or because we have shifted slightly away from our original vision. The exercises in *The Breakthrough Experience* can re-energise jaded leaders, enabling them to review where they are in their personal life and checking how that aligns with their daily reality.

We want to create a *growth mindset* in ourselves and in other entrepreneurs. This is a combination of:

- Positivity

- Agility

- Abundance

- Resilience

More than that, the entrepreneur destined to go beyond start-up into significant lasting success also needs to cultivate the attitude that gets things done. This includes the learnt skills of planning, managing and problem solving, and possibly the hardest skill of all: letting go of the small stuff, ie, the ability to delegate.

Emotional and mental health support

The need for emotional and mental health support in business has gained greater significance since the pressures of Covid, during which greater numbers of entrepreneurs struggled emotionally and reached out for specialist counselling. There is a global increase in levels of depression, with the increase especially high in South Africa.[8] We therefore need to factor support into any activity such as business acceleration, where people are under extreme pressure.

Recognising the importance of mental wellbeing starts by selecting entrepreneurs with resilience and the inner strength to recover from unforeseen crises. These can come in many different forms, including divorce, fractious partnerships and loss of key clients; large-scale circumstances, such as wars or economic downturn; or acts of God, such as floods, pandemics or droughts. By providing access to professional mentors, support groups, and specialists such as counsellors or psychologists, we can reduce the likelihood of burnout or depression and increase the likelihood of long-term success.

In South Africa, and in many other economies where traditional values are still very strong, women leaders can find themselves under additional pressure. Their business role will conflict with expectations from family and community for women to be at home, playing a traditional supporting role. This can cause significant marital and family challenges for female entrepreneurs, adding to the already stressful role of entrepreneur. Under these circumstances, special support – in the form of female peer groups, special discussion groups, and exposure to female role models – can be helpful.

In South Africa's 'born free' generation, where taking a safe and respected government or corporate position is considered the gold standard, men also struggle to break away from the high or unrealistic expectations of parents and grandparents, who cannot understand their choice of entrepreneurship as a career.

Summary

Mindset is the critical starting point of entrepreneur success. From experience, we know we can support and enhance existing leadership capabilities, but we cannot change the deep-seated nature of an individual. Not everyone is an entrepreneur by nature, so to grow successful small businesses at scale, it's important to be sure that we select people with strong entrepreneurial talents.

Thereafter, our job is to understand and support individuals' personal passion and purpose and help them to stay aligned with those as the business grows. A leadership that is self-confident and self-aware, passionate, focused and happy has a much greater chance of success.

Key takeaways

- We need to understand mindset as it relates to entrepreneurial success. A resilient mindset is needed to endure the many challenges that business presents.

- It's important to understand the different types of entrepreneurs and to select those with the right attitudes and aptitude for growth.

- The journey of any small business can be tough, and entrepreneurs may need support to overcome emotional burnout and depression.

- Additional specific support may be needed for women and for others battling with the conflict of traditional or cultural beliefs that clash with their business role.

3
Method

Whilst once-off success can happen randomly, to achieve consistent success, you need a method – a system that allows you to repeat the recipe that baked the cake. This is the reason top athletes develop and stick to meticulous training methods, bookkeepers and accountants use consistent methods, and successful businesses build systems into their operations. These systems and methods are the building blocks for growth. They enable an entrepreneur to take their individual skill and replicate it. For the same reason, accelerators need systems and methods in their setup and operations.

The business plan

Common wisdom taught in business school is that everything starts with a business plan, yet in truth the lengthy process of perfecting these plans often gets in the way of progress. It's my observation that many a great business idea has been stalled by multiple attempts to first perfect the business plan. In a start-up, the business plan is more like a dreamy intention than a formal plan. At this formative stage of the business, a quick sketch of the idea and a first action plan is usually sufficient.

To illustrate this (and if you are an ardent business plan fan, perhaps skip this bit), our first case study reflects my own personal experience.

CASE STUDY: An agile start

I started my first multimillion rand business with no business plan at all. My husband and I were living and working in Lusaka, Zambia – he as a farmer and I as agricultural economist for Zambia's Commercial Farmers Bureau – when an overnight change in Zambia's financial system suddenly allowed citizens to access foreign exchange.

This was a major change for a socialist country in those days, prior to which the Zambian government controlled everything from the price of maize and bread to the allocation of import licences. Before the change, you couldn't walk into the bank to pay international invoices, and you needed permission from the government to exchange kwacha for dollars. As a result, operating any business that needed imported items such as building fittings, window frames, spare parts for vehicles, or the vehicles themselves was a real challenge. The old system privileged a few with access to forex. Overnight, the new foreign exchange auction system opened access to everyone in the country.

We spotted this as a business opportunity and within a week had taken advantage of the new gap in the market. We had zero knowledge of forex trading, auctions or importing, but we did have a willing market in our extensive network of Zambian farmers – an entire sector of buyers with decades of pent-up demand for imported goods.

We quickly repurposed an existing farming company and launched into the import business. Over the next few years, this unplanned start-up rose to become a multimillion-rand import–export business serving a wide client base. The simple truth is that had we stopped to research, write business plans and investigate all the risks, we would have been frightened by what we didn't know, or we would have paused so long to think and plan the business that the opportunity would have passed us by.

Today, I still maintain that a start-up entrepreneur needs only an understanding of the opportunity and a simple action plan. This agile mindset allows them the freedom to test, adjust and prove the idea first, and thereafter to build a business or investment plan to attract the partners and finance to grow it.

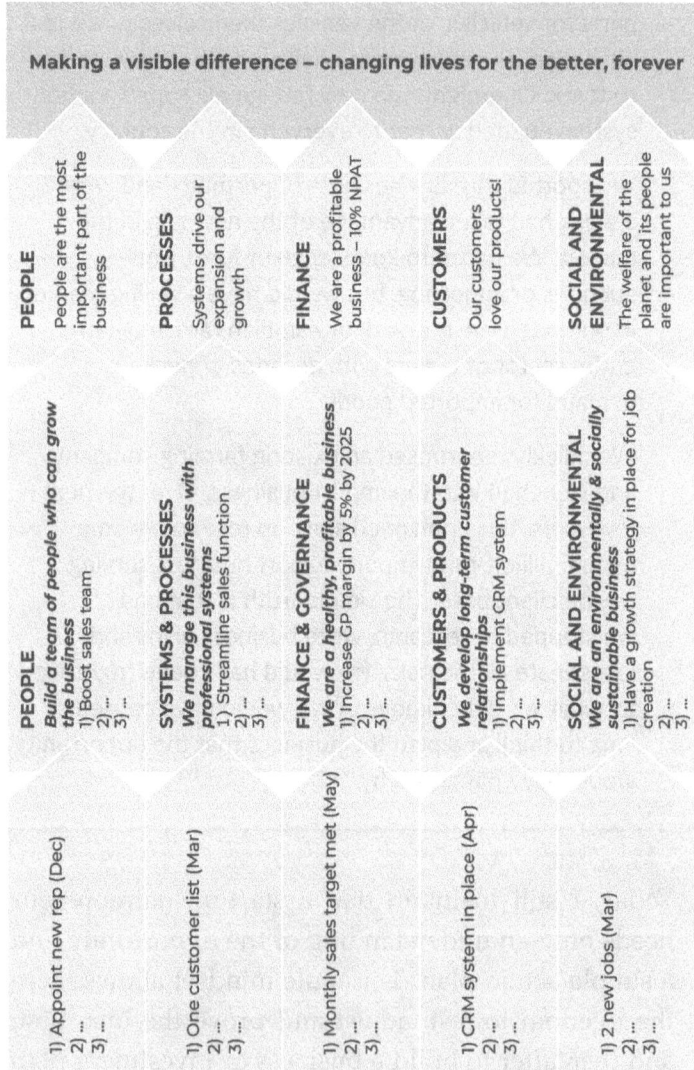

VISION

Making a visible difference – changing lives for the better, forever

FIVE PILLARS	STRATEGIC OBJECTIVES	KEY PERFORMANCE INDICATORS (KPIS)
PEOPLE People are the most important part of the business	**PEOPLE** *Build a team of people who can grow the business* 1) Boost sales team 2) … 3) …	1) Appoint new rep (Dec) 2) … 3) …
PROCESSES Systems drive our expansion and growth	**SYSTEMS & PROCESSES** *We manage this business with professional systems* 1) Streamline sales function 2) … 3) …	1) One customer list (Mar) 2) … 3) …
FINANCE We are a profitable business – 10% NPAT	**FINANCE & GOVERNANCE** *We are a healthy, profitable business* 1) Increase GP margin by 5% by 2025 2) … 3) …	1) Monthly sales target met (May) 2) … 3) …
CUSTOMERS Our customers love our products!	**CUSTOMERS & PRODUCTS** *We develop long-term customer relationships* 1) Implement CRM system 2) … 3) …	1) CRM system in place (Apr) 2) … 3) …
SOCIAL AND ENVIRONMENTAL The welfare of the planet and its people are important to us	**SOCIAL AND ENVIRONMENTAL** *We are an environmentally & socially sustainable business* 1) Have a growth strategy in place for job creation 2) … 3) …	1) 2 new jobs (Mar) 2) … 3) …

Plan on a Page (developed using the ec@aps methodology)

Too many book-learnt business specialists drive the business-plan-first philosophy and push aspiring entrepreneurs to sweat over theory, register a business name, and sign up with the tax department before they take even the first step to action. In my experience that process simply doesn't match the reality of 90% of business start-ups. More than anything, entrepreneurship requires action. As Richard Branson so rightly says, business needs you to *just do it*![9]

Plan on a Page

The simple, action-orientated Plan on a Page is ideal for start-ups and early-stage entrepreneurs. It was introduced to us by Clive Howe from ec@ps, and we gratefully acknowledge his methodology.[10] It is a beautifully simple, condensed plan, midway between a 'back of the cigarette box' sketch and the weighty but often inappropriate 100-page business plan. This plan includes a written reminder of the guiding business purpose and vision, and highlights key priorities and actions to get there. Its power is in its simplicity.

The Fetola Success Wheel

Entrepreneurship is a fully immersive experience, requiring leaders to be dynamic in their decision making and to have the courage to step daily into the unknown.

In contrast with traditional, linear tools, the Fetola Success Wheel illustrates the business growth journey in a 360-degree circle. It acts as a reminder that every time a business rolls forward, its needs and priorities change. Typically, when we solve a problem in one area, it causes another one to arise elsewhere. For example, landing a big sales deal will put pressure on staffing, add challenges to the regular supply of raw materials and almost certainly strain the cash flow. Nothing is without its consequences!

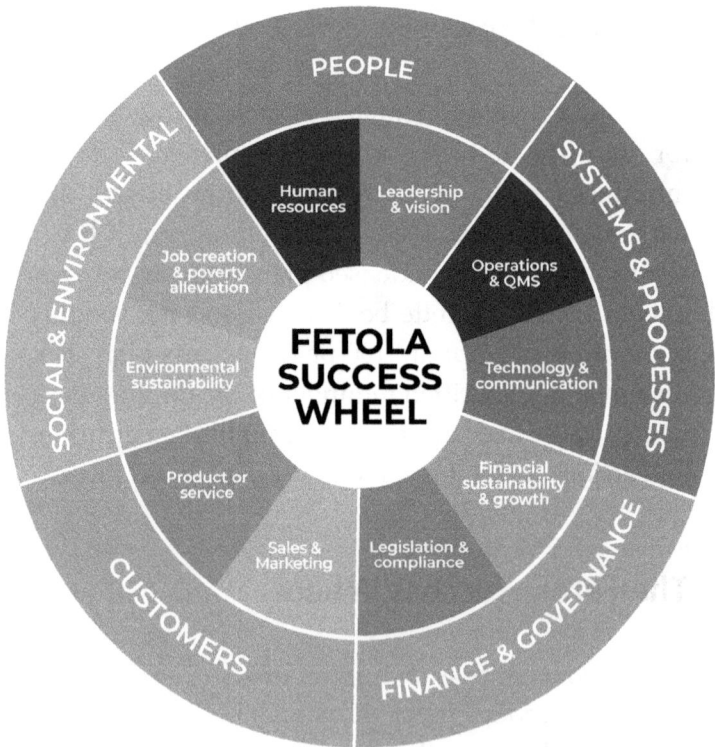

The Fetola Success Wheel

Assessing before action

The starting point of the growth journey is a thorough assessment of where the business is now. In the case of a start-up, this will be an assessment of the leadership team, their reasons for wanting the business, and the concept or idea itself.

It's best when the entrepreneur conducts their own business assessment and identifies their own strengths and weaknesses, thereby feeling fully engaged in the assessment process.

As most leaders are by nature competitive, there will be a natural tendency for them to want to score the business highly to get the best result. Rather than seeing this as a flaw in the assessment process, the self-assessment should be used as a basis for a discussion between the entrepreneur and their mentor. In this way, both parties gain a closer knowledge of the underlying human stories and realities behind the score, leading to deeper understanding and alignment of the journey that lies ahead. Only when there is alignment can the task of acceleration truly begin.

Metrics and performance management methods

The maxim *What you measure you manage* is a fitting reminder for both the entrepreneur and the accelerator team. Deciding what to measure requires careful thought. It can be tempting to want to measure every moving part of business performance, but it's better to decide on a few meaningful measures and track them consistently.

It's also important that the measurements are meaningful to the person tracking them. Otherwise, they will likely lose interest and either simply stop tracking or enter fictitious data just to tick the job as done.

To get this process right, we need to do the following:

1. Choose data that is easy to collect and verify. For example, it's easy to measure and verify monthly sales, but it's trickier to measure and validate profit, which is an outcome of multiple variables. Similarly, it's easier to measure electricity usage by looking at the meter reading or adding up the bills than it is to measure net carbon emission, which is a hugely complex process of multiple interlinked factors. Well-chosen, easy-to-collect data is far more likely to be collected consistently and recorded correctly, which is key to success.

2. Make the process worthwhile for the data collector by asking them to measure data that has a meaning and usefulness to them. This immediately increases the likelihood of collection consistency and accuracy. The difference between *This data helps me to run my business more effectively* and *This data collection is a painful waste of my time*

doesn't need further explaining, yet how many times do we load people with data-collection expectations, neither explaining nor considering this? Data that is useful for the entrepreneur in making critical decisions, which is fed back in the form of graphs and comparison with others in the sector, increases the chances of success.

3. Ask the questions:

   - *What will I or we do with this information?*

   - *How will knowing this make an impact?*

   - *If I had to choose between question a or question b, which is more important?*

Rather than burdening everyone with collection of marginally useful data, we can streamline this to a selection of important drivers and, where needed, add further rich detail through case studies.

Essential business systems

Before we move on from this chapter, I want to add a few words on the essential systems and methods entrepreneurs need within their business. This could be a book on its own, so I'll deal only with some of the basic principles.

As I have said before, systems and methods are the building blocks for growth of any business. They are the way to ensure consistent processes across a team and ensure consistent quality as the business expands.

Systems ensure standard ways of working throughout the business, through production methods and quality management processes. In the early-stage business these can take the form of a simple worksheet or checklist taped to the wall, which increases in complexity according to need.

The first system most businesses need is a set of standard roles and responsibilities, job descriptions and ways of working so that the founder can step away from doing everything and recruit people to replicate required skills. A centralised customer relationship management (CRM) system usually comes next, as the business seeks to hire a sales team and needs to share data and information on clients and potential customers.

Digitisation of the business processes adds a critical layer of effectiveness, and there are many free digital tools and apps for the small business. Digitisation can be as simple as creating an online booking calendar, adding an email signature to AI chatbots and automating sales on an e-commerce website.

Summary

This chapter has discussed the importance of clear and simple methods in the business.

It has shared useful planning tools for small businesses and considered the never-ending cycle of changes, illustrated by the Fetola Success Wheel.

The overarching theme of the chapter was about starting by assessing the gaps and opportunities of the business, aligning expectations before acceleration. We were reminded of the importance of performance measurement, both for the SMME and the programme as a whole. The chapter concluded with a quick review of some of the important systems a small business needs.

Key takeaways

- Systems and processes are the foundation of business growth.

- A brief, prioritised business plan that can be easily understood and shared with your team helps to ensure clarity of purpose. A simple plan on a page makes priorities visible.

- The Fetola Success Wheel helps to remind us of the continual motion of the business and encourages us to ask important questions in all 360 degrees of the business.

- The starting point of the acceleration journey is to assess the business with a gap analysis, before aligning expectations and agreeing an action plan.

- Performance management is essential to monitor and adjust progress of the accelerator. It's best to select a few meaningful key performance indicators that are easy to verify.

- Collection of complex or difficult data will result in inaccurate results, whereby entrepreneurs either fail to report or make up the information.

- The use of technology to improve efficiency in the business is becoming the norm. Even small businesses in rural areas can be encouraged to identify and use technology-based solutions that match their needs.

4
Market

In many ways the most challenging component of the business growth process is mastering the market segment. The word *market* is used here as a catch-all phrase for all the aspects of market readiness, finding buyers and making successful sales. It covers the important starting point – a clear understanding of the target market – and includes commentary on personal and business branding, social media presence, advertising, e-commerce, market introductions and more. Market readiness and market access is a critical part of the growth journey and one where many entrepreneurs – and many accelerator programmes – struggle.

The reality is that without buyers willing to purchase what you are selling, there is no business. Sadly, many entrepreneurs start their business with a burning desire to produce without really understanding who their ideal client is or how they are going to sell to them. This is *supply-side thinking*, where all the focus is on what can be produced or supplied. A successful business needs to be driven by market demand, not by what the business wants to sell.

My own experience of this was in the early 2000s. Many hundreds of women in rural South Africa were encouraged to use their traditional beading skills to produce necklaces, bracelets and earrings, beaded mats and beaded home décor. Unfortunately, this well-meaning drive was created without a proper assessment of market demand for such traditional products, and that demand was weak and quickly saturated. The end result was that garages and rural homes were filled with large stocks of unsold product made through the hard-earned labour of these women. This is a perfect example of the perils of supply-side thinking.

Subsequently, this production system has become much more refined, with a few specialist producers successfully targeting high-end home-décor consumers and others producing exclusive African-styled accessories.

Fetola's VIP Market Access Model includes the acronym VIP as a reminder that this is indeed a very important player in the business growth mix. V stands for Visibility of the brand, I for Introductions to customers, and P for Product–market fit.

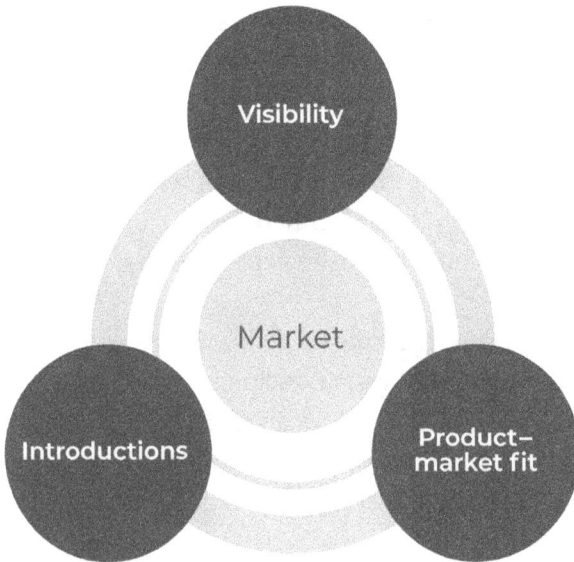

VIP Market Access Model

Product–market fit

Although the P comes last in VIP, *product–market fit* is the starting point. Identifying exactly which market is the right fit for the product or service is critical. It seems such a simple concept, yet many entrepreneurs have only a surface understanding of their ideal market and weak insight into their customer needs. Often the answer to *Who is your ideal customer?* is vague, generalised and undefined. This broad definition dooms the small business to failure when pitted against established organisations that dominate the market.

To succeed, small businesses need to try and dominate a micro niche in the market. Businesses that operate in a market where they lack recognition and respect find it difficult to differentiate themselves and can easily be out-competed on price. In contrast, by identifying and owning a clearly defined segment of the market, they can become the go-to expert for that segment.

A tight, clear target-market focus in an area of strength is a much more powerful recipe to solid business success. Think traditional African remedial tea, not just tea. Think planet-friendly, handmade outdoor furniture with a lifetime warranty, not just outdoor furniture.

Another common mistake many early-stage entrepreneurs make is identifying products or services that meet a pressing customer need, but despite this apparent demand, their target customer lacks the money to make the purchase. A good example is given in the following case study.

CASE STUDY: There's a gap in the market, but is there a market in the gap?

Ubuntu Training Solutions is run by Gloria Mbethe, (name changed for anonymity) an ex-teacher and passionate youth community champion. She is rightly concerned about the poor level of maths education in rural areas, where many learners fail to grasp important mathematical concepts.

To solve this, Gloria created a business providing maths tutoring to impoverished township schools. She has rightly assessed that, as education is poor in the townships, there is a high demand for quality education solutions.

Sadly, though, the business is not taking off. Whilst there is lots of demand for Gloria's solution, her target population lacks money to pay for private tuition, no matter how good it is. She has identified a market demand but not a viable business opportunity.

This kind of tricky problem is ripe for social enterprise – finding ways to solve critical education, health care and related services where they are needed, but where poverty is a barrier to purchase.

Partnerships with corporates and the government – for scaled access and low-cost health-tech and ed-tech – is needed to circumvent the commercial realities and provide alternative revenue models and to ensure success.

Product pricing, quality and reliability

A review of the product–market fit leads to a conversation about product price, quality and reliability. In our globally competitive world, where so much is made in China and the East, many local small businesses struggle to produce their products at a similarly competitive price. The standard response can be for entrepreneurs to throw up their hands in despair and accuse the buyer of wanting to exploit them. In reality, the reasons for a mismatch could be many, for example:

- Their production methods are inefficient

- Wastage is a problem

- Their raw material costs are high

- They lack understanding of their costing and pricing

- Their products are overengineered

Overengineering – where product quality is better than needed – results in products that are too expensive for the market. This can be solved through product re-engineering, to redesign products to meet expected quality and price points.

Product and business process re-engineering is a powerful way to reduce waste of all kinds. In manufacturing especially, process re-engineering is a valuable tool, whereby a specialist engineer radically redesigns the business processes to achieve dramatic improvements in productivity, cycle times, quality, and employee and customer satisfaction. Designing out waste in this way can reduce cost of production and is a key component of the circular economy business model, where waste is eliminated in production, reuse and repair. If re-engineering is not possible, then the entrepreneur may need to walk away or rebrand, moving into a more luxury segment and marketing the additional quality to a different client base.

Visibility – building a profile

Once the product has been optimised for the chosen market, the next step is the V in VIP – *visibility* – optimising the brand message, brand reputation and reach. To be successful, a business needs to be visible, and visible to the right audience.

A support team can do a lot to help the business refine and professionalise the business message and brand collateral in line with their target market.

Storytelling is a valuable tool, and small businesses can use origin stories of the founder to provide a unique differentiator. In this way, we can help entrepreneurs to create a category of their own. The business Cabinet Works is a great example of this, as outlined in the case study below.

CASE STUDY: Reaching new heights

Cabinet Works founder Andy de Klerk was frustrated by the slow growth of his bespoke cabinet-making enterprise. The company was making top-end, high-quality fitted kitchens and bespoke furniture, yet they could only command a mid-level price. It was clear from the market analysis that, to move up a category, they needed to rebrand and reposition.

When I looked into kitchen companies, they all looked the same. Every website was similar, and a kitchen was a kitchen – all companies had much the same offering. Andy is not average, though. Behind his quiet demeanour, he is a world-class mountain climber, with Mount Everest and many of the world's other major peaks under his belt. Not your average kitchen man, that's for sure!

With this in mind, we helped Cabinet Works rethink their brand, using powerful elements and visuals from mountain climbing. We also linked in features of successful mountain climbing such as planning, precision, quality, safety and building a grand vision.

This unique story allowed Cabinet Works to build a differential, and it elevated the brand into a class of its own – one that appealed to their top-end customers, who also aspire to climb mountains and live adventurous lives.

Cabinet Works moved swiftly away from its position as an unknown mid-range kitchen company, and it is today the premier cabinet-making company in South Africa. Andy remains a quiet, out-of-the-limelight type of guy, but his story helped position the company in a class of its own.

Activities such as this benefit businesses in a number of ways, including:

- Helping the entrepreneur find and own a unique niche and then professionalise, optimise and extend their reach

- Increasing leadership (and stakeholder) confidence

- Providing valuable assets that support sales and marketing efforts

Branding basics

The art of branding is ensuring that the brand (which includes the look and feel of the colours and logo, the business name and its core message) clearly portrays the ethos of the business and its product and service offering.

The more authentic and memorable a company's branding, the better results it will achieve. It's very easy for graphic designers and entrepreneurs to get this wrong. The design team can fall into the trap of creating a corporate identity that is perfect for a fantasy company but not for the company as it truly is. Whilst a level of brand aspiration is good, authenticity is vital. A misaligned brand message can break client trust, so this is a red flag to avoid.

A word of caution: when brand building, entrepreneurs often obsess about the logo, spending hours on design and redesign. How many logos – other than McDonald's, Nike and Twitter – can you actually recognise, though? In reality, it is the name that we remember, not the logo. The company name is everything, and it is possible to get this wrong, as illustrated by our original name!

The full registered name of Fetola is actually Fetola Mmoho – a wonderful descriptive Sesotho name, meaning *changing together*. Great concept, except that the vast majority of people do not speak Sesotho and find it difficult to say or spell. This problem became clear to me a year or two into the business, when I realised that our name provided negative branding (if there is such a thing). Everyone – including me – did their best to avoid saying it. Our name was clearly bad for business. By simplifying Fetola Mmoho to Fetola, we were able to transform the tricky tongue twister into a unique and memorable, globally recognised name. Lesson learnt!

Introductions and market access

After establishing a strong profile, the business must get in front of (and be noticed by) their ideal customer, yet many start-ups have weak networks and lack the skills to do this.

There are three primary ways for the accelerator team to overcome this:

1. Specialist teams can teach entrepreneurs how to build their own visibility in buyer networks, using digital marketing tools, social media, events and relationship building.

2. Mentors can share the power of their networks and facilitate introductions.

3. Professional marketers help to match buyers and sellers in high-value transactions such as corporate or government supply chains. Professional relations with procurement

managers, together with education on the complexities of trade at this level, are invaluable to the emerging entrepreneur.

Building the market pathway

Another word of caution here: whilst everyone loves stories of overnight success, in many cases these stories ignore the long, silent journey of growth that led to success. People can therefore mistakenly believe in instant success – that a start-up only needs access to market, and the bigger the better.

In practice, fast-tracking an emerging enterprise into a sophisticated corporate value chain will not succeed if the entrepreneur overestimates their experience and the readiness of the business. Corporate supplier development initiatives are designed to bridge this gap by providing hand-holding to the emerging entrepreneur. This handholding needs careful consideration, as the risks to company reputation and revenue from onboarding unprepared, small suppliers can be considerable. This is why many supplier development programmes focus on non-essential or non-core products and services. For example, a cleaning services mess-up is just an irritation, but a failure in supply of essential production components will impact profitability and quite possibly corporate reputation as well.

A healthy economy has a thriving business-to-business ecosystem, where small businesses have many opportunities to trade with each other. This ensures that they grow their skills and climb the market ladder in stages, learning as they go and improving quality, systems, staffing and cash flow management skills along the way. This stepwise journey prepares the small business for the pressures they will face when they reach the sophisticated and often unforgiving national or global supply chain.

Bigger also isn't always better, and many entrepreneurs have found themselves worse off after landing their dream deal. To illustrate, let me share the story of Glenda, an entrepreneur with a passion for gardening.

CASE STUDY: Bigger isn't always better

A few years ago, Glenda (name changed for anonymity), who had learnt to propagate and grow succulents in her back garden and ended up with too many, decided to turn her hobby into a business. She had started giving them away to friends and family, who were so enthusiastic that she took a stand at the church Christmas fair. Not only did she run out of stock, but she also had a pocketful of cash to pay for the family Christmas holiday.

Coming back from holiday in the New Year, she decided to book a spot at the monthly farmers' market, which meant that she had to streamline her propagation system and increase her output. She quickly attracted standing orders from the local gift shop.

Two years later, Glenda was supplying a regional gifting company. She had employed staff, who used simple checklists to ensure consistent quality in the production, packaging and delivery of the plants. A bookkeeper managed the accounts and the online payments and ensured that all the orders were paid before shipment.

When Glenda's success story was featured in the local press, a friend connected her to a buyer at two national retailers, and all hell broke loose. The large orders and strict deadlines mean that she battled to meet their demands for consistent supply of quantity and quality. There was also the added demand for regular certificates of health and safety on workers, premises and even her suppliers. The computer systems for delivery dates and windows for delivery times allow no room for error, and the payment terms went up from a happy COD to payment 120 days after delivery. On top of that, she had to pay for shelf space and absorb the cost of damages and unsold items. The business went quickly from profit-making fun to a cash-strapped, loss-making nightmare.

Getting ready for the big time

To successfully engage with large-scale national or international corporate supply chains, the small-business entrepreneur will need to master six further factors:

1. Networking and relationship building

2. Costing, pricing, negotiating and contracting

3. Volumes, guarantees and delivery schedules

4. Payment terms, cash flow management and financing

5. Packaging, barcoding and SKUs

6. Quality management, quality systems and compliance

Let's take a closer look at each.

1. Networking and relationship building

People do business with people they know, like and trust. The most successful sellers are therefore those with the ability to find and nurture professional relationships with buyers. This means understanding the decision-making structure within the chosen business or sector, identifying the decision makers, and becoming comfortable with relationship building at this level.

There is no point wasting effort in wooing a junior employee or transformation manager if all decisions are made by the CEO or the buyer. This is where formal supplier-development training is useful; and mentors, peers and trade partners can provide a bridge. It is not a step that can be skipped.

2. Costing, pricing, negotiating and contracting

Corporate buyers are paid to beat down the price of products and services they purchase. Confidence is critical when negotiating with buyers, and entrepreneurs need intimate knowledge of the cost and break-even points of their products. Without this information, they cannot know if the offered price is acceptable, which is hugely disempowering in any price negotiation.

Comparative competitor pricing, quality and terms of offer will add power to these negotiations. For example, if the seller offers reliability, local materials and rapid delivery and knows these are key factors for the buyer, those elements can be used to bargain for a higher price. Similarly, understanding the relationship between price and quality can lead to conversations on re-engineering to match quality with the required price point.

In contracting and drawing up legal agreements, where the greater power of the corporate legal team dominates the small supplier, advice from contracting specialists can assist.

3. Volumes, guarantees and delivery schedules

These often create a stumbling block for a small business wanting to make the leap into major supply chains. Going from supplying a small local retail shop to feeding regional or national supply chains is an exponential leap in production and may be too much for one business.

It's here that collaboration amongst small businesses can be a useful strategy. It is used successfully, for example, in the South African fruit industry, where South–South (South Africa / South America) growers formally collaborate to ensure continual supply to the European market, despite individual challenges that one country or supplier might experience. The continual supply guarantee helps defend their position and price in the market.

4. Payment terms, cash flow management and financing

It's here that many businesses fail, as larger orders require more working capital, tight cash flow management, and access to order finance. Agreeing to long payment cycles can spell a death knell for under-prepared small businesses. This is especially challenging when entrepreneurs agree to already paper-thin margins as the cost of bridging finance wipes out profit margins.

The acceleration team can help entrepreneurs to recognise this risk by modelling the cash flow impact of large orders and then use this information to negotiate better terms or know to walk away from the deal.

The accelerator's investment readiness team is there to assist by educating the entrepreneur, helping them to prepare a professional investment pack, and matching the entrepreneur to appropriate finance providers.

5. Packaging, barcoding and SKUs

Where large retailers run automated warehouses and inventory systems, these require absolute compliance from suppliers. Errors can be costly to the relationship and bank balance.

The acceleration team can assist the entrepreneur in understanding and complying with these packaging and warehousing needs.

6. Quality management, quality systems and compliance

These are vital at this level. Many large corporates monitor and publicly report their quality compliance and are hugely sensitive to the cost and consumer-trust impact of poor quality. SHEQ (safety, health, environment, quality) systems include but are not limited to ISO 14001, OHSAS 45001 (previously ISO 18001) and ISO 9001.

The acceleration team can help entrepreneurs identify and implement quality systems that will transform the professionalism and marketability of the business.

Summary

This chapter has highlighted market-readiness models and tools designed to solve the critical component of access to markets for lasting business success.

It began by discussing product–market fit, which is a vital component of business success. This includes assessment of the product–market fit, identification of a viable niche market, and the journey of growth up the market value chain.

Having identified a clear target niche market, the next step is to build the visible profile of the business, including the creation of a unique company brand and authentic brand message.

The section on introductions outlined the importance of networks and the value that mentors and peer connections can bring in providing information and introductions to new markets.

The chapter included a cautionary section on the dangers of force-feeding success by fast-tracking small businesses into demanding and sophisticated corporate value chains, and it provided examples of more sustainable market growth models. The short section on product re-engineering illustrates how to improve market appeal and retain profit margins.

The chapter ended with some key tips to advance a business into the next level: the national value chain.

Key takeaways

- Building a unique and appealing brand is more than just a logo. It is about the whole brand message, including the way you do business; the brand, colour, logo and name; and the repeat stories you tell.

- Without sales there is no business, yet many emerging entrepreneurs lack the necessary networks and market access to reach their ideal customers.

- Accelerators can provide market access in three ways: by teaching skills to entrepreneurs, through introductions facilitated by mentors, and through professional matchmaking and partnerships.

- Many entrepreneurs fail to understand which market they are in, believing that everyone is their customer.

- A healthy economy is one in which there is a thriving small business and B2B ecosystem. This provides the learning grounds for emerging businesses to gain the experience needed to become part of a supply chain.

- Fast-tracking emerging enterprises into sophisticated supply chains can result in devastating failure. Close supervision and support are essential.

- Small businesses should identify and master a micro niche that they become known for. In this way they can build thriving businesses and defend against competition.

5
Money

No one starts a business with the intention to lose money, and yet this is often the outcome. The goal of good acceleration is to flip this around and ensure that the business exits in a better, more robust and more profitable state than when it started. From a financial management perspective, this essentially means helping entrepreneurs to become comfortable with money, produce accurate monthly accounts, manage cash flow, and use their management accounts as a tool to monitor performance. From an institutional investor's perspective, this means de-risking small businesses by deploying catalytic funding mechanisms that integrate pre- and post-investment support.

The main aim of acceleration is to prepare the business for growth. This encompasses better management of the money in the business, and the ability to success-fully raise further growth investment. This financial focus may seem obvious to the institutional or impact investor, but it is often not so clear for the entrepreneur.

The bottom line in business is money – no money, no business. It's surprising, though, how few entrepreneurs in the African ecosystem focus their skills and efforts on mastering their money. Many a good business fails to grow – or indeed fails altogether – because of this. Money in our context encompasses all the elements that stack up to a profitable business, embracing everything from personal attitudes to money, accounting and financial management to investment readiness and fundraising.

Acceleration teams look for leaders with an abundant mindset and help them to build on this confidence to create profitable, financially sustainable businesses. We also implement catalytic investment funds, providing early-stage enterprises with affordable access to growth finance.

The emotions of money

Money is both a logical numeric science, in which numbers either do or don't add up; and an emotional, behavioural concept, in which cultural, personal and familial belief structures have a strong yet often intangible influence. Financial advisors divide their clients into two broad categories: the risk takers and the ultra-cautious. In business both extremes are a red flag – too much appetite for risk leads to gambling decisions, and too little appetite for risk constrains the business with fear.

Although some entrepreneurs are comfortable in dealing with money, many are not. Unblocking subconscious negativity around money starts with identifying the entrepreneur's personal, emotional relationship with money, and the influence that family and upbringing have on the belief system. Interactive workshops and coaching are useful tools. Also helpful are simple personal finance strategies such as recording and monitoring spending, writing and sticking to grocery shopping lists, and reducing the number of family credit and store cards.

Many financial management books are written for the converted. Some – like Ntando Maseko's book *Welcome to Financial Freedom* – use simple guidelines for everyday use.[11] These include not spending more than you earn, curbing wasteful expenditure such as entertainment, and staying out of the debt trap. It is this kind of advice that is needed as a starting point to heal personal relationships with money.

The importance of accounts

For accountants and those who love numbers, it seems inconceivable that an entrepreneur would run a business without carefully recording their transactions, maintaining monthly accounts and monitoring financial performance, but it happens more often than we might like to imagine.

My own personal experience was exactly like this, in the first import-export business my husband and I started. The business quickly grew from a bright idea into a dynamic enterprise with a turnover of millions, yet for the first three years we had no proper accounting system. We were so focused on the operations of the business – caring for clients, generating sales and building the core of the business – that we neglected our accounts.

Three years into the business and needing to raise capital for expansion, we tried to piece together the financial history to create a passable set of management accounts. This was when we recognised that we needed to reorganise the business and employ a quality bookkeeper and accountant. Whilst it feels a bit embarrassing to have to admit this, it is very common for small businesses to run for years without a set of books, only to realise later with shock how important those are. During the Covid pandemic, thousands of entrepreneurs suddenly realised they were unable to access grant funding relief for this reason.

The lesson here is that – if not yesterday – now is the best time to get serious about financial records. Entrepreneurs find it easy to be busy doing other things, but there will come a turning point when the business needs to produce financial records, which may well be too late.

Financial records are an essential starting point, but it doesn't stop there. Unless the entrepreneur can understand and interpret the management reports presented by their bookkeeper, and ask questions of clarity, then they are still running their business with blindfolds on. The task of the accelerator support team is to remove the blindfolds and build an enthusiasm and skill for sound financial management.

Financial management

In South Africa, in 2023 only 6% of learners passed higher grade maths with 60% in grade 12, therefore a great number of entrepreneurs are especially weak in maths.[12] Some have been so traumatised by their school experiences that they actively avoid numbers. Women in Africa are traditionally excluded from maths and science subjects at school, making them especially vulnerable in this area.

To turn this around, at all touchpoints the accelerator team needs to generate an enthusiasm and energy around money and an aura of delight around financial management. A powerful two-step approach is as follows:

1. Get entrepreneurs to imagine themselves in the future, looking back at the important actions they need to take to reach success.

2. Walk a journey with them on which they acquire the financial management skills and confidence to build a successful business.

The basic need is a reliable, efficient financial record-keeping system. In its most simplistic form this can be a set of paper record books for income and expenses, and a file for slips and bills. A dedicated business bank account ensures that personal expenses are separated and drives the right attitude.

Ideally, automated accounting tools make financial record keeping easy, efficient and error-free. Compiling all sources of information – including cash, mobile payments and online transactions – into a complete set of records builds up the full picture of the business.

To make business decisions, the growing business needs access to regular, accurate financial information. Understanding how to analyse the monthly management reports is essential. As the business grows, entrepreneurs need to track and manage their performance – profit ratios, overhead trends, cash flow forecasts and sales performance are key.

Access to monthly, accurate records is important, but I am not a fan of entrepreneurs trying to manage their own bookkeeping unless this is a natural skill and genuine interest for them. It is important, though, that these records are accurate, up to date and closely interrogated every month (or more frequently, as needed) by the entrepreneur.

Good financial training is a critical component of empowering confident business leaders. This should be pitched at the right level and resonate with the entrepreneur to build enthusiasm, confidence and skill.

CASE STUDY: Financial education

My personal finance journey illustrates the experience of many other entrepreneurs. In my case, despite having a business-related degree, I still felt ignorant when discussing company financial reports. I was too afraid to ask questions in case this revealed my ignorance, and I would sit silently at the boardroom table, feeling disempowered and inadequate.

To remedy this, I decided to study for an MBA. I am now still far from being an accountant, but I have the confidence to ask questions for my own clarity and understanding.

Most importantly, this confidence puts me in a position to access and interrogate the information I need to make sound business decisions. This is this level of empowerment that entrepreneurs need to feel.

Investment readiness

Let's be frank – one of the biggest challenges around investment readiness is the communication gap between entrepreneurs and investors. Each group moves in its own world of understanding, expectations and norms. The average entrepreneur doesn't speak banking, and the average banker doesn't speak small business. For this reason, our investment readiness process includes four steps:

1. Investment education

2. The investment proposal

3. Pitch preparation

4. Deal negotiation

Let's look at each in more detail.

1. Investment education

The first task of the investment readiness team is to help educate the entrepreneur in the language of the investor, explaining:

- Investment terminology

- The different types of finance and investment deals

- What investors are looking for and why

This helps the entrepreneur to identify the right type of investment and guide them in preparing a sound proposal and pitch. The process is hugely empowering, as the entrepreneur gets to understand their business and their finances in the eyes of others.

It's worth noting the emotional journey that entrepreneurs make when stepping from self-funded growth to external debt or equity finance. For many this represents a huge mindset leap, taking them from the comfort of self-funded business growth, where they are fully accountable only to themselves, into a future that is dependent on and tied to others. This loss of autonomy is a step not all entrepreneurs are prepared to take.

Sensitive, open-ended enquiry may be needed to understand this reticence and work through entrepreneurs' underlying concerns. Try to avoid a situation where the investment readiness team is focused on achieving their own targets. Forced growth will most likely result in high anxiety and poor leadership decisions, resulting in weak post-investment performance.

2. The investment proposal

Building on the improved understanding of investment readiness, the entrepreneur and acceleration team need to identify suitable investors, using investment-assessment matching tools such as those provided in the templates section. This helps to improve the success rate by reducing mismatches.

Creating a good investment proposal can be challenging for the average solo entrepreneur, which is one of the many reasons many early-stage businesses struggle to access finance. The proposal is both a marketing document and a meticulous factual record of financial and business evidence, requiring multiple layers of skills and understanding. It's no easy task to craft a good investment proposal that speaks to the needs of the investor. It should ideally contain:

- Pertinent information on the business's past, present and future state

- Details about the business's compliance, personality and unique market potential

- Technical content

- The business revenue model

- Evidence of financial viability

- A risk assessment

- A profile of the entrepreneur and the team

The investment request or 'ask' should also be clearly stated, along with supporting return-on-investment and cash flow projections.

3. Pitch preparation

Once a match with an investor has been identified, the practical development and presentation of the business pitch itself begins. It's here that the entrepreneur has to encapsulate their business value into a single document to showcase its investment value.

The most successful pitch decks are often those developed by the entrepreneur, because they are then highly personalised and charged with the vitality of passion and purpose. In addition, the closer the entrepreneur is to the deck, the more empowered they feel to make critical decisions during and after investment pitching. However, because these investment pitches are often highly technical and beyond the skill of the average small-business owner, our professional assistance is often needed to build one.

4. Deal negotiation

The prize at the end of the investment readiness journey is a successful finance deal that works for both parties. The investment team guides the entrepreneur in identifying suitable opportunities, negotiating the term sheet and closing the deal. This often warrants the involvement of financial experts, to help prepare realistic cash flow projections, provide market knowledge and the negotiation skills needed to secure favourable financial terms.

Unaided, many entrepreneurs agree to deals that satisfy an immediate need for money, whilst putting them on course for failure due to unrealistic repayment schedules, or interest rates that they cannot service due to weak profit margins. The investment team is there to bring calm, rational thinking to ensure the deal creates lasting value and builds relationships that contribute to the sustained financial success of the business.

Once again, it's important that this process leaves the entrepreneur with greater confidence in their knowledge and skill, feeling empowered to take the business into the next stage of growth. A professional investment readiness team ensures that this confidence shines through in the entrepreneur's pitch.

Access to catalytic finance

Globally, there are thousands of impact investors seeking to invest billions of dollars into emerging African small businesses. However, a structural gap exists in the R250,000–R5 million ticket size, where access is either unavailable or exploitatively expensive.

In emerging economies such as these in which Fetola works, resolving this gap is crucial to successful transformation of the economy. This is an area in which we are actively engaged, working with local and international partners to build blended finance solutions that support the small-business success we all seek.

Personal wealth

No section on money would be complete without acknowledging the importance of personal money habits on long-term success.

If our job is to help build the entrepreneur's business, it may seem counterintuitive that we also encourage them to build independent wealth. Given the rigours and challenges of small business, though, having a safe nest egg can calm and motivate the entrepreneur. Sadly, a great number of entrepreneurs invest all of their resources into their business, only to see them evaporate if the business fails. A strategy to regularly carve off and save a portion of profits enables the entrepreneur to build personal wealth, which can be a reassuring insurance strategy. This strategy should include the necessary boundaries and legal ring-fencing to protect the separate asset in the event of business failure.

My personal experience of losing everything many years ago comes to the fore here. I went from owning multiple businesses, houses, cars, boats and the like to standing with only the clothes on my back and three children to feed. That trajectory makes me ever conscious of the need for personal wealth planning. Whilst the ultimate causes of the business collapse were out of my control, our poor personal investment behaviours and our failure to separate family from business finances meant the failure of our businesses brought us to zero. An entrepreneur will gain peace of mind from the knowledge that their personal wealth is growing and safe, independent of the business.

Good mentors who are well-matched to their entrepreneurs are adept at identifying these often-subtle issues around money and have the ability to address them appropriately.

Summary

Money is a powerful driver of success. Learning how to make and master money is critical to the health of the entrepreneur and the enterprise. This chapter covered the topics of financial management, financial understanding, investment readiness and personal wealth. It also contains a reminder that capital raising is just one of a suite of actions needed to ensure successful business growth, and that internal efficiencies that build lasting business resilience form the strongest foundation.

We touched on the importance of ensuring that the accelerator team is in touch with the needs of the entrepreneur, who may be weak with numbers and not really interested in finances.

Too often, the glory boys in the small-business world are those who lend the money – the venture capitalists, the banks and the impact investors. In this chapter we reminded ourselves that there is a cost to growth and all investments come at a price. We stay focused on a whole-health approach.

Key takeaways

- Access to finance is a critical success factor for emerging businesses. It is possible to solve shortfalls with catalytic finance solutions, integrated with pre- and post-investment support.

- The acceleration team can help entrepreneurs recognise mental and emotional blockages behind unhealthy attitudes to money and engage more positively with their finances.

- Financial record keeping, in the form of accurate monthly accounts, is a basic requirement in any business, yet this is often the least perfect part of a business.

- Without verifiable financial records and annual financial statements, a business will struggle to access finance, conclude advanced deals or enable beneficial partnerships.

- Most entrepreneurs enter acceleration believing that money is all they need. The process of investment readiness can reformulate this thinking towards a healthy 360-degree story about the business.

- Investment readiness – including preparation of business plans, investment proposals, cash flow forecasts and the like – is a specialist skill that the acceleration team can provide. The most successful outcome is where the entrepreneur has been supported to prepare their own investment deck.

- A healthy entrepreneur is one with a diversified portfolio of investment. Encouraging entrepreneurs to build separate personal wealth improves their self-confidence and reduces anxiety when times are tough.

6
Mentorship

*W*here *is my mentor?* That is the familiar cry of many an entrepreneur as they battle with unknown challenges and frustrations.

Mentors can make or break a business, and many successful entrepreneurs are eager to credit the roles their mentors played in their success. As the mentorship component of an acceleration programme is often the most significant element – and mentoring can quite literally make or break a business – the choice, matching, training and management of mentors is something we absolutely need to get right.

In the entrepreneurial environment, it's important that mentors are themselves avid learners, always seeking to improve their own knowledge and contribute their relevant wisdom and experience.

A small business can also gain value from an experienced corporate executive, provided that person is sensitive to different entrepreneurial realities where resources may be lacking, decisions have to be nimble, and structures are often looser and less process driven.

Over the years, I have formulated and worked with a set of guidelines that ensure mentoring empowers entrepreneurs to:

- Solve their own problems

- Gain wisdom on where and how to access the support they need

- Become confident enough to ask the right questions

The Fetola way of mentoring actively also avoids creating dependency, which is such a common problem in this sector. Our mentors have learnt how to act as guides, encouraging and supporting the leadership to run their own race instead of stepping into the business to fix things. This can be frustrating for mentors, who are often by nature 'fixers' and itch to jump in and make things happen. The result, though, is that the entrepreneur gains confidence in their own ability and feels empowered to act rather than feeling overly impressed by the mentor's skills and intimidated by their own apparent relative weaknesses.

This 'stand alongside' mentoring method is illustrated in the following example, which highlights the importance of experience, training and mentor support.

CASE STUDY: From township to major retail

Thandi Mazibuko had been running a thriving small business, supplying local customers and the occasional tourist for a few years, when she secured an order from a national retail store for her handmade Christmas gifts. Once the excitement of receiving this big order had died down, the realisation set in of just how big a job it would be.

To meet the complex and precise purchasing and warehousing needs, the gifts would need to be manufactured, packaged, prepacked and barcoded, and delivered at a precise time and to a predetermined order schedule. This was a big stretch for a small company used to much smaller orders in less formal markets.

The mentor's first instinct was to jump in, take over discussions with the buyers and manage all the intricacies of the delivery chain. Had he done so, though, the buyer relationship would have transferred from the entrepreneur to the mentor, creating a dependency and sending a subconscious message to the entrepreneur that she was not up to the job. Whilst the order would be successfully completed this time (a win), the entrepreneur would feel disempowered, and dependent on the mentor for future negotiations and orders (a loss). The success story would then simply be a flash in the pan, and the business little better off in the long run.

The mentor, who had hands-on experience in similar situations from his own business, was able to show restraint and stand alongside the entrepreneur, supporting her by reviewing and guiding her with communications, assisting in the smooth running of the manufacturing process, and providing support through the complexities of packaging and barcoding the products. He also helped her to ensure the correct and timeous delivery to the warehouse, whilst educating and empowering Thandi and her team.

Despite the high-pressure stakes, the order was completed successfully, and the entrepreneur gained experience and confidence from the process.

Professional mentorship

The pace at which the mentor applies their growth strategies needs to be closely aligned to:

- The circumstances of the business
- The real-life situation of the environment
- The potential, purpose and growth pathway of the leader

This concept of pace is embedded in our PACE mentoring system, which stands for Professional mentorship, Acceleration tools, Connect to networks, Empower and educate.

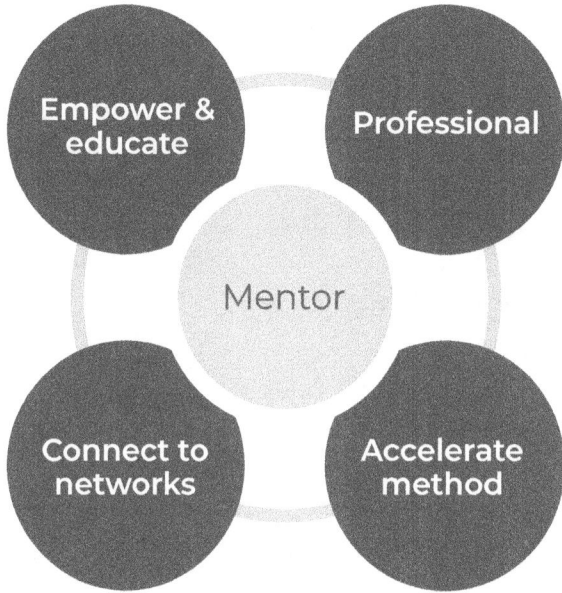

Mentorship PACE model

It's very easy to get this wrong. Sitting on the sidelines of a business, a mentor may see the huge potential and get carried away with grand plans, only to realise later that this strategy is misaligned with the goals of the business owner, who could simply want their business to succeed enough to put his kids through school. The opposite is also possible, of course. Occasionally, mentors might misread the potential and passion of entrepreneurs whose goals and dreams seem unrealistic, putting the brakes on rather than accelerating their growth.

Over time we have built mentoring methods that train the mentor to first assess each individual business. They can then match growth and acceleration strategies to the business model, the leadership ambitions, the vagaries of the market and expectations of capital raising. We use planning tools such as gap analysis, milestone setting and growth targets to optimise individual mentoring strategies.

Mentor qualities

A key component of professional mentorship is the ability to connect entrepreneurs into value-adding stakeholder relationships, which can be further enhanced when mentors are connected to each other and able to pool their knowledge and networks.

Professionalism goes beyond formal training or certification – a mentorship qualification does not guarantee a good mentor. Other key components include:

- The ability to do what is right for the business

- Putting ambitions and ego aside, to ensure that the guidance given is empowering to the entrepreneur

- Supporting with advice that is valuable, relevant, realistic and ethical

Despite every effort to match personalities, the truth is that not all mentors are always loved by their mentees.

This is partly because the role of a mentor is to bring about change, and change can be a painful process. Mentors need to be adept at change management and able to build a climate of mutual respect that strengthens the entrepreneur's self-confidence and inspires them to move the business forward.

When looking for mentors, it's sometimes easier to identify what you don't want, and you don't want someone that is too full of themselves and their own sense of importance. A weak mentor might also be someone who lacks empathy and misses the all-important personal aspects that hold people back. They might also come from a different environment and lack self-awareness. A weak mentor might also be someone who lacks hands-on and relevant entrepreneurial experience, whose book-learning is therefore out of touch.

A good mentor, on the other hand, is confident in their own skin, has both IQ and EQ, and seeks specialist assistance for challenges beyond their own ability.

Mentor selection

There are five different types of mentors and advisors:

1. Volunteer mentors

2. Peer mentors

3. Generalist mentors and sector specialists

4. Group and remote mentors

5. Consultants and technical advisors

Let's look at these different roles in more detail.

1. Volunteer mentors

One benefit of using volunteer mentors is tapping into a huge pool of individuals with the desire to make a difference. It is also a great way to test out mentors before taking them on full-time. Voluntary participation is dependent on people's time and levels of enthusiasm, but great success can be achieved, as shown in our Covid-pandemic response.

CASE STUDY: Mentor hotline

During the 2020 Covid pandemic, we successfully launched a volunteer mentor support programme, in partnership with a local South African bank, to provide free online support and advice to entrepreneurs.

Mentors had to pass a short online test and were provided guidelines for their behaviour. Using an online matchmaking tool, the platform then matched technical experts to entrepreneurs and enabled quick access to online support.

An enthusiastic response from willing volunteers, who were keen to support local business owners, meant that we received applications from 605 volunteer mentors. We also accumulated 857 entrepreneur registrations.

The online platform worked during the height of the pandemic as a quick advice tool, providing valuable technical and other support.

---

2. Peer mentors

Peer and alumni mentors are also a great asset, as the entrepreneur can be matched with a like-for-like individual who has walked the same journey. These mentors can use their own accelerator journey experience to guide and support. We have found a great willingness amongst our alumni to pay it forward in this way.

3. Generalist mentors and sector specialists

Generalists and specialists bring different sets of skills. It is helpful to have a foundation of strong generalist mentors with hands-on experience across a range of sectors, who are masters in 'the business of business'.

As the complexities and growth ambitions of the business increase, these need to be supplemented by sector specialists. This blend allows for a good generalist mentor to request support to supplement their own advice, for example, from a specialist in financial modelling, agriculture or the export market.

4. Group and remote mentors

In an ideal world, every entrepreneur should be supported by their own on-site mentor. Where this is not possible, either due to location or budgetary constraints, group or remote mentoring can provide a good alternative. The value of group mentoring is the opportunity for entrepreneurs to learn from each other, but this is weighed against the lack of privacy or ability to delve deeply into the individual business.

Remote mentoring provides a cost-effective way to match mentor and mentee, no matter their location. Its challenge is that it can be harder to build relationships and foster trust and deep understanding online. Tools such as video calls and conscious interpersonal processes such as personal checkins can assist.

5. Consultants and technical advisors

We often need to explain to entrepreneurs the difference between mentors and consultants or technical advisors. Whilst mentors provide guidance support from the sidelines, consultants and technical advisors are contracted to play an active role in the business. Examples include skilled individuals delivering legal and contracting advice, HR specialist services, or help with process re-engineering.

Added value

One of a mentor's important roles is to introduce the entrepreneur to a relevant market access and support networks. These introductions provide a route to fresh opportunities and can actively support business growth.

I'm also a firm advocate of mentor upskilling, which is critical to the ongoing improvement of quality. As the world rapidly changes, mentors also need to constantly develop their skills. Providing access to new knowledge, and encouraging cross-sharing insights and experiences, helps to build the collective wisdom of the mentor team and raises the quality of mentorship provided.

Mentoring can be a lonely and stressful job, and a support group can boost emotional wellbeing and provide a sounding board for ideas and opportunities. Our mentor groups provide emotional support and a fun place to 'hang out'.

Summary

Mentorship can change the trajectory of a business. Our role is to ensure that this course change takes the business to a safe harbour, not onto the rocks. Ensuring you have a team of high-quality mentors, matched to the right business and able to deliver exceptional results, requires resource planning, mentor–mentee management and an ongoing focus on improvement.

In this chapter we were reminded of the symbiotic nature of the acceleration process, which has to proceed at the right pace – not too slow and not too fast. This begins by matching the experience and wisdom of the mentor to the potential, purpose and growth pathway of the entrepreneur. A mentor who tries to force their agenda onto an entrepreneur can do more harm than good. Conversely, a mentor who is insecure or unsure of the growth rate of the business can unfairly hold it back.

We discussed the importance of matching the type of mentoring to the task at hand and compared the roles of volunteer mentors, peer mentors, group and remote mentoring, generalists, sector specialists, and technical advisors. Mentors are there to provide support from the sidelines, whilst a consultant dives into the business and delivers work that makes things happen.

The power of mentor support groups and the potential that introductions have in opening markets was also outlined. Lastly, we covered methods for empowering and educating mentors through upskilling to ensure that they constantly develop as a critical growth team resource.

Key takeaways

- Quality, professional mentorship is one of the most powerful components of an acceleration programme and needs to be carefully planned and managed.

- Good mentors inspire the entrepreneur with self-confidence.

- Mentorship is a multi-faceted skill, involving the ability to assess the needs, desires and fears of the entrepreneur, and the problems and challenges of the business, and to help the entrepreneur to navigate their way to success.

- Matching the right mentor to the business leader takes into account the personality, culture, experience and skills of both parties. The mentor management team helps to ensure support to both parties, especially in dispute.

- Mentor selection, training and ongoing support ensures the best mentors are retained in your acceleration team.

- There are many different types of mentors, including volunteers, peer mentors, group and remote mentors, generalists and specialists.

- Mentors are different from consultants and technical specialists.

- Highly valued mentors are those with industry networks that provide connections for market access, finance and other skills.

7
Skills Training And Peer Groups

I have discussed the support tools and methods we use to provide wraparound support to the business as it grows. In this chapter I will discuss the use of practical skills training. By sharing relevant and practical business skills, and showing entrepreneurs how to apply this in their business, we can help them to take their business to greater heights. Training works best when it matches the needs of the individual entrepreneur and their sector, education level and stage of business. When combined with the support and stimulation of active peer groups, this benefit is further deepened.

Skills training in an acceleration programme is about raising awareness, changing attitudes, and embedding new methods of finding and resolving challenges. It is deliberately challenging and uses action learning to embed new ways of thinking.

Training provides critical thinking points, to awaken the entrepreneur to gaps in their knowledge and give direction on ways to bridge these gaps.

Getting training right

As an entrepreneur, I'm conscious of the need to deliver tangible value at all times. Time is money for entrepreneurs, and it's our responsibility to make sure that the time we take from their working day brings them lasting benefit. This means focusing on content that is applied, practical and relevant. It is often different from the theory-based entrepreneurship training provided in education institutions.

Ideally, this skills training also encourages deep learning, which comes from engaging in a 'struggle' with the content, not just from being fed facts. This deep learning goes beyond the transient memory of fact recall, and it transforms into a full understanding of knowledge and how to use it in decision making.

Ultimately, the purpose of accelerator skills training is to make entrepreneurs think differently and in an agile, flexible and innovative way. Our job is to equip the leader with the thinking skills needed to adjust their strategies and action plans as they build their business.

This is an area I personally enjoy, and I find you can only write and deliver truly effective content if you have experienced the challenge yourself. I do this by imagining myself as one of the entrepreneurs in the room and asking the question *If I was this person, why would I care?* This helps to cut out irrelevant course content and keeps the focus on what is truly game-changing.

It's important to adjust training content to the needs and wants of the audience. Inserting case studies that match the culture, industry, stage of business and aspirations of your audience is one way to do this.

Accessibility

Training content needs to be delivered to the entrepreneur in the way that best suits them. This affects decisions on how to train – is it best delivered in groups, one on one, classroom or debating-style? Is it best online and managed or self-service and self-learning?

All forms of training need to be easy to navigate and well laid out. Online material should be easy to find and simple to access, and in the preferred format, for example, Word templates, PDF, interactive online checklists, podcasts or video. Consider if the audience prefers short or long videos and check if the speaker is clear. Are there subtitles for those who are hard of hearing?

These days there are many tools to meet these varying needs, from self-service online videos and user-friendly learner-management systems to simple, graphic-rich checklists. Where data is very expensive or internet connection weak, content must be available in low-data versions, available in offline mode, or provided on a data-free learning platform.

Most entrepreneurs are time-poor, so it's important to focus on information that is of the highest practical value with the greatest positive impact. When writing content, ask yourself *What is most important?* and then cut out the rest.

Additional rich information can be provided in supplementary learning content or reading lists.

Even more important than the content is the style of delivery. A facilitation style that encourages entrepreneurs to engage in the struggle of learning, inspiring them to battle with the problems and concepts in the training room, ensures that they come away with:

- An appreciation of the problem

- The need for a solution

- A good grasp of how to find and solve the problem

Most successful is a facilitation style that creates a safe space for learning, whilst encouraging two-way debate. A room full of entrepreneurs will contain experts in many different forms, and a skilled facilitator will mine that resource, creating a rich and inspiring learning experience for everyone.

A teacher–pupil style of training or lecturing is seldom appropriate for entrepreneurs. It can be disrespectful to their position as leaders, and ineffective as a means of generating deep and lasting understanding.

Whilst certificates can be a nice motivator, the critical learning 'certificate' for entrepreneurs is a change in thinking and the altered behaviours they take back into their business.

Team training

It's important that entrepreneurs are encouraged to provide training to their own teams. Skills transfer is a critical component of building the depth of management layer needed to move the business to the next stage of growth. There is nothing more frustrating for an entrepreneur than coming away from a great training workshop with a head full of knowledge and then not having the time, skills or resources to pass it on to their key staff.

Accelerators can help here by allowing additional team members to participate in training sessions, and for mentors to include this in their checklist for engagement. Training workshops can also be recorded, with workbooks, templates and guidelines provided.

Networking and peer groups

One of the most transformative moments in my own MBA was when the class was asked to plot the size and value of their personal and professional networks. Up until that moment, I had firmly believed that my value sat in my intellectual skill and knowledge, which I had carefully nurtured. I was shocked to realise how small my network was in comparison with others, and with this came appreciation of the value of a strong network. For those with natural skills in networking and friend-building, this value is obvious. For others, networking takes practice and conscious effort.

Entrepreneurs who come from families where there is no prior experience of business ownership, where their community have no understanding of the rigours of business ownership, often feel isolated. Their fears and anxieties fall on deaf ears, and the entrepreneur even at times comes under attack, leaving them feeling stranded and alone.

Being accepted into a group of like-minded people with similar stories to tell can be a relief, allowing the entrepreneur to relax and share and receive support. The purpose of accelerator peer networks is to create this sense of belonging and support, and a sense of pride for the entrepreneurs, one another and the accelerator.

The ideal peer group is a space where each participant can feel seen and heard. This is especially important for women who come from traditional or patriarchal societies and face a double challenge, as entrepreneurs and as women. When gender bias is an inhibiting factor to their success, female-only networks can be of value.

Ideally, the group should contain a sufficiently diverse range of people to allow rich learning and collaboration, and some light-hearted fun. When this works well, the friendship bonds founded in accelerator peer groups are often sustained long after the programme is over, with these friendships becoming an anchor for entrepreneurs as they grow. It can be extremely rewarding to find a new network of friends who share a similar experience and ambition.

Summary

Skills training is vital to help the entrepreneur to be successful in business. In this chapter we have considered ways to make sure the training content, format and delivery are right for each individual and each business. Given the leadership role of entrepreneurs, the teacher–pupil style of lectures or classroom learning is seldom appropriate, and a more empowering method of engaging debate delivers better results.

A strong peer group is part of the culture of an acceleration programme. Good peer groups are highly valued by entrepreneurs – as an emotional anchor, a source of information, and access to opportunities and lasting friendship.

We know from our experience in Fetola that this doesn't just happen by accident. Value-adding peer networks require conscious effort, using the appropriate levers to create and support these communities.

Key takeaways

- Entrepreneurs are pressed for time and want to learn applicable skills they can use in their business.

- Acceleration is a practical, applied process, not a theoretical skills training course.

- Engaging facilitation, interactive discussion and applied learning result in the best outcomes for entrepreneurs.

- Accelerator peer groups are often the one place where entrepreneurs can engage with people just like them. These groups provide friendship, emotional support and guidance, and they can result in lifelong friendships.

- Strong peer-group connections can help to foster business partnerships, exchange information and improve success.

PART TWO
ACCELERATOR CASE STUDIES

N ow well established and applied across many sectors, we use the methods, models and the theory of acceleration outlined in Part One as the basis to design our accelerator solutions for the continuously changing needs of small businesses. The aim is to ensure that accelerator programmes deliver on their promise and consistently deliver above-average, lasting impact.

In Part Two I'll bring all that theory to life with practical examples of accelerators we have designed and implemented. The intention is to show you what works, what doesn't, and why. This is where the rubber hits the road, as they say, so I'll do my best to share some of the magic.

The case studies include:

- An online accelerator for ideation and start-up

- A sector-specific example, using the circular economy

- Social enterprise

- Post-disaster recovery

- Our rural and township models

Each accelerator case study is shown in two parts: first, the Fetola accelerator model, followed by an example of an entrepreneur journey within a specific accelerator.

8
Rural Accelerator

Since our first accelerator back in 2007, we have had a strong focus on helping small businesses in the outlying and rural areas of the country succeed. This is where there is so much need for support, but given the challenges, these areas are not such a popular option for most acceleration teams, who tend to cluster in the urban areas. Having studied agriculture to the Master of Science level myself, and with my personal history embedded in agriculture in Zambia and South Africa, I have a deep connection with and interest in the success of rural communities. Given this, and our history in Fetola, it's not surprising that our series of case studies starts there.

In South Africa, as in many developing parts of the world, rural poverty is of great concern. The increasing attraction of the modern city, with its promise of riches, means that young people are leaving for the cities in increasing numbers. This leaves sparsely populated, increasingly poor and underserved rural communities, where without inherited wealth and family farms to make a decent living, the opportunities are few.

This chapter's case study shows the rural accelerator programme in its current form as it operates successfully in all corners across rural South Africa.

Overview of a rural accelerator programme

The case study at the end of this chapter focuses on the Fetola rural accelerator programme – a fully serviced wraparound accelerator for early-stage and established enterprises.

All participants in our rural accelerator are previously disadvantaged (black, in accordance with the national BBBEE strategy to redress Apartheid injustices). The accelerator is free to participants, bar a small commitment fee, and is highly sought-after. Intake is oversubscribed by up to 100:1 each year.

MINI EXPLAINER: The BBBEE policy

South Africa's Broad-Based Black Economic Empowerment (BBBEE) policy aims to promote economic transformation and empower historically disadvantaged individuals, particularly black people, women, and persons with disabilities. It seeks to achieve this through measures such as preferential procurement, skills development, and ownership and management equity targets, among others.[13]

The intensive, holistic rural accelerator uses all aspects of the Fetola Growth Method discussed in earlier chapters and is implemented over an eighteen-month period. This includes a three-month probation period in which candidates are tested on their suitability. There is an emphasis on women, youth and entrepreneurs living with a disability and a strong focus on selecting businesses that are job creating.

The accelerator is designed for enterprises from all provinces across the country and from a mixture of industry sectors. Given the rural focus, there is an emphasis on agriculture, manufacturing, forestry and rural services.

Acceleration comprises non-financial and financial support. Core non-financial support is made up of standard components that apply to every entrepreneur such as:

- One-on-one mentorship

- Six interactive and practical two-day business skills workshops

- Peer group and accountability group participation

- Access to the learning management portal

- 24/7 personal support from the acceleration team

Additional needs-based solutions are individualised and delivered on request. These include a complete range of growth tools, from personalised brand building to process re-engineering and psychological support.

Ongoing personal feedback and performance monitoring via the online FTPortal enables entrepreneurs, mentors and other stakeholders to monitor progress in real time. Ongoing use of data insights from this personal feedback and performance monitoring are used by the accelerator team to inform actions and guide progress.

Financial support is provided in the form of grant investment. Businesses apply for grant finance, which is provided on review and assessment of the impact potential of the grant. Extensive support in the form of financial readiness and coaching is provided, to help entrepreneurs understand and apply the basics of investment mindset to receive and manage the grants.

The problems we are addressing

Rural economies represent a cluster of challenges. Addressing them requires an approach that acknowledges and finds solutions to logistical and cultural barriers, as highlighted below.

1. Urbanisation

Many challenges in rural communities arise from the loss of skilled individuals, especially the youth, to the cities. Over the last ten years, urbanisation has increased across developing economies, especially in Asia and Oceania, where the urbanisation rate rose by almost 7% from 44% in 2012 to 50,6% in 2022. Africa saw a 4,6% increase in the same period.[14]

Urban migration is driven by the lack of access to basic services such as health care, education, clean water, and sanitation. This results in poor health, low literacy rates, and limited opportunities for employment in the rural provinces. Weak road and rail infrastructure further hinders movement, which in turn limits the income potential of farmers and rural business owners.

2. Cultural challenges

Patriarchal belief systems also tend to be more dominant in the rural provinces, with historical limitations for women's access to education and business own-ership, and perpetuating gender-based poverty and inequality. Young girls without education face a dire future. Without access to employment or the skills and liberty to start a business, they are faced with the only option to marry, and often at a horrifically early age.

In deep rural communities, where there is a lack of exposure to both employment and entrepreneurship, some households have never experienced the world of work, let alone had a business owner in their midst. Entrepreneurs from such families can face great chal-lenges when breaking out from the norm to start their own businesses.

The vision for success

The vision for the rural accelerator is for entrepre-neurs to:

- Gain the self-confidence, skills and resources to start and build successful businesses

- Become contributors to healthy rural economic growth, shared wealth, and local job creation

A thriving, rural business has the potential to make a significant economic and social impact. The creation of a job in this environment has a far-reaching and greater impact than a job created in the city, where many opportunities abound.

More than that, when we build and strengthen a local ecosystem or value chain of rural businesses, we create a mechanism for money to circulate from business to business.[15] This generates wealth within the rural community rather than wealth escaping out into the corporate value chain and back to the city.

One of the great tragedies in modern South Africa is the lack of impact that social grants have made in rural communities. For example, in the Eastern Cape 2,8 million citizens receive social support in the form of grants.[16] Despite this injection of money, the province still has persistently high rates of poverty. Little or none of this social grant money remains circulating in the local economies, as there is very little local small business activity. Latest data shows that the Eastern Cape has only 172 333 SMMEs, or one for every sixteen social grant recipient citizens.[17] In comparison, the most economically lively and wealthiest province of Gauteng has a much more active small business ecosystem, with one small business to every three grant recipients.

The challenge is to increase the number of active small businesses in rural areas such as Eastern Cape and build thriving local economies.

What makes it different?

The Fetola rural accelerator is unique in its combination of non-financial and financial support. This combination enables consistent high performance and lasting impact in areas where few others succeed.

One example of the rural accelerator model is the SAB Foundation Tholoana Enterprise programme. Independent long-term impact studies show that 95% of graduates are still in business years after graduation. The programme is regarded by many as the leading accelerator programme in South Africa.[18]

The programme uses the full range of the non-financial support in the Fetola Growth Method, including professional mentoring, entrepreneur-led skills training and extensive individually customised attention, to ensure the diverse businesses receive solutions that are tailored to their needs.

In addition, the provision of grant finance is critical to unlocking early-stage growth. In a country where access to early-stage finance is nearly impossible to obtain, and where entrepreneurs from disadvantaged backgrounds lack access to personal wealth, this grant finance is a game changer. Grants are provided in a managed environment that demands clear business motivation, financial management and the meeting of performance milestones. A strong focus on financial literacy, financial management and the building of long-term business health helps to optimise lasting impact.

In addition, lifetime relationships are retained with the entrepreneurs, who can join the alumni support programme and apply for further support and loan finance after graduating from the accelerator.

This programme is implemented via a decentralised hub-and-spoke model and supports entrepreneurs located many hundreds of kilometres apart from each other.

MINI EXPLAINER: The hub-and-spoke model

The hub-and-spoke model is made up of a central hub or core team that delivers its activities via several smaller spokes or teams. The hub is responsible for defining the project's goals and objectives, allocating resources, and overseeing the overall progress of the project. The spoke teams are responsible for carrying out specific tasks or activities related to the project.

Benefits of the hub-and-spoke model include:

- Increased efficiency
- Better coordination between teams
- A more streamlined decision-making process

However, it also requires effective communication and collaboration between the hub-and-spoke teams to ensure that the project progresses smoothly and meets its objectives, and between spoke teams to ensure consolidated cross-learning.

Unlike city-based entrepreneurs, who have had exposure to advanced education and corporate work experience and may even come from families in which entrepreneurship is the norm, many rural entrepreneurs are the first in their family to start a business. Their success requires that these unique challenges are understood, and that mentors, trainers and project managers come from similar or matching backgrounds. Our ongoing mentor skills-transfer and support programme helps to upskill local mentors and achieve consistent quality of a high standard.

Critical success factors

To be successful in such a challenging environment, the rural accelerator needs to get a number of things right. As we are investing resources – time and money – into entry-level businesses operating in a challenging and therefore risky environment, it's important to select the right entrepreneurs. These are leaders with strong entrepreneurial skills and the resilience, grit and courageous leadership needed to push through inevitable adversity.

Not all business models are viable in this environment, so it's important to select those that fit. Typically, this includes businesses that:

- Use abundant local resources such as farming and forestry

- Take advantage of gaps in the market such as in bakery, butchery or transportation

- Use unique local skills to manufacture goods destined for national or export markets such as basketry, food processing or even furniture

Importantly, the business's investment or financing needs must align to the availability and size of the grant. For example, this excludes a farm that needs large capital investment to expand; but it would include a bakery requiring a new oven to meet orders from the local retailer, as a step towards provincial expansion.

What can go wrong

With many moving parts in an intensive and high cost/return accelerator such as this, when things go wrong, the social and financial costs can be significant. Let's look at some of these costs.

1. Early exits

Despite all efforts, the occasional mismatched entrepreneur can slip through the cracks. It can be frustrating for everyone when expectations are not met, and if financial and staff resources are used up on a poorly performing business, this represents a potential lost opportunity for the programme. It's for this reason that this accelerator programme has an extended probation period, with clearly defined milestones, so mismatched businesses can be identified and sensitively exited.

Factors out of our control such as unexpected illness, divorce or family challenges do happen. Whilst solutions such as additional mentoring and coaching support can help to mitigate some of these effects, some early exits cannot be avoided.

2. Market access

Access to markets is a fundamental challenge in marginal rural areas, where local consumer buying power is weak, and transportation costs are high due to distance and poor roads. Adding to the burden, these areas are frequently overlaid by weak cell phone coverage and power outages.

Success requires skilled mentors who have experience in generating success in such conditions and can deploy effective solutions for building market opportunities. Introduction of e-commerce and the use of market aggregation are powerful tools.

3. Access to staff talent

Access to qualified staffing talent is a challenge in many emerging economies, especially in rural areas. South Africa, specifically, suffers a shortage of technology, science and maths-based talent as schooling in these subjects is weak. This means that basic financial literacy skills are poor.

In addition, as the brightest brains migrate to the cities for work, the availability of specialist staffing talent in rural small businesses can be extremely challenging. Fortunately, since Covid the concept of remote work is better accepted, and specialists can often be brought into a business on that basis.

4. Cultural barriers

As illustrated in the case study below, the rural accelerator programme faces challenges when traditional values and expectations conflict with the methods of the business. For example, a farmer may start cultivating in a manner considered taboo. As recently documented on film, this happened in Burkina Faso, where farmer Yacouba Sawodogo introduced his Zia method of planting into pits filled with compost outside of the traditional planting season.[19] Although ultimately successful, he faced hostility and even violence for many years before his improved farming methods became accepted.

Traditional expectations may also demand entrepreneurs to employ relatives, give favours to local dignitaries, or frown on women in positions of leadership. Resolving such challenges requires professional community engagement. A forewarning of this problem is an important part of selection, as deeply embedded resistance can completely scupper the potential of a rural business.

5. Communication challenges

Communication is more likely to go wrong in an accelerator that operates across diverse and remote rural locations. Distance, language barriers, weak access to internet and differences in cultural norms and expectations can lead to misunderstandings. Use of technology that is appropriate to the receiver and extra care in ensuring communications are simple and clear help to ensure messages are received as anticipated.

CASE STUDY: Rural entrepreneur – manufacture to national distribution

In this case study we look at a rural participant in the SAB Foundation Tholoana Enterprise Programme. The Tholoana Programme is a long-term initiative to improve the social wellbeing of rural South Africa, with a focus on job creation in businesses owned by youth, women and people with disability. We highlight an exciting youth-owned business that is bridging the urban/rural divide by manufacturing in the rural community and selling into a national market.

Puleng Johannes Motupa is a young socially minded entrepreneur from a small rural village in Limpopo, who manufactures and markets innovative products into the local communities.

His inspiration for starting his business, Motupa PJ Enterprises, was to find solutions for the people in his community who struggled to afford electricity. As a result, young girls had to walk long distances to fetch firewood for cooking. In response to this need, Puleng came up with an idea to manufacture a heat locker box – a non-electric slow cooker that can cook for up to twelve hours at a time. This product also reduces carbon dioxide emissions from traditional wood fires and allows community members to save money on paraffin costs.

The Tholoana Journey

On joining the SAB Foundation's Tholoana Enterprise Programme, Puleng set revenue growth as a primary goal. During the eighteen months, he was able to list his business on two national e-commerce platforms and retail his signature non-electric slow cookers. This breakthrough was a huge milestone for the business, creating much-needed brand awareness and kick-starting rapid growth.

The accelerator team also assisted with rebranding of products and finetuning the packaging material to best suit the online market. As a result, the business secured additional long-term, high-value offtake agreements.

In readiness for the anticipated growth of the business, Puleng and his team invested in developing their systems and processes to enable them to serve a multitude of retail stores. During its eighteen-month growth period, the business grew in revenue by more than 500% and increased employee numbers from eighteen to twenty-five – a significant impact for a rural village where few other opportunities exist.

Two years after Puleng graduated from the Tholoana programme, the business continues to grow strongly. Motupa PJ Enterprises has secured new national deals and sales into the US, Canada and Mexico, with Europe and Dubai in the pipeline.

Summary

A healthy economy is one where all communities are fed and well resourced. This requires a balance of urban and rural wellbeing, with thriving small-business ecosystems across the country.

I am especially keen on helping small businesses in rural areas, as this is often where help is most needed and the challenges are greatest. The impact of a successful small business in marginalised rural areas can be significant. It creates an anchor around which other enterprise can flourish, and where unemployment is rife and opportunities are few. Even one business with one additional job is worth its weight in gold.

Female role models take on greater significance in areas where traditional norms and values don't embrace the success of women in business. A slip-stream is created, encouraging young girls to finish high school, study further and empower themselves as independent adults.

Building successful enterprises in these marginalised areas is not always easy, and a carefully crafted acceleration programme is required. The vision – for empowered entrepreneurs and healthy local economic ecosystems – makes it so important to get these small-business accelerator programmes right.

Growth strategies that work here may make no sense in the cities, and vice versa. The skills needed by the professional team of mentors, coaches and growth partners are different, and extra patience may be needed from all stakeholders working in areas where things move more slowly.

Careful selection of entrepreneurs with the right attitude and aptitude, identification of viable markets, and access to growth capital are the starting point of success.

The successful rural accelerator is one in which women, youth and people living with disabilities participate in core growth modules and receive personalised support, targeted at their specific needs. Access to growth capital, in response to well-motivated applications; additional financial training; and support to establish sound financial behaviours in the business help to ensure lasting success.

Key takeaways

- Unique challenges in rural areas require teams and mentors with personal experience and understanding of the local situation.

- Rural businesses often face higher costs due to logistical constraints such as poor roads, distance from markets and lack of infrastructure.

- Weak or non-existent internet and cell phone connection make even the simplest of communications challenging and exclude rural businesses from modern interconnected markets.

- The combination of non-financial support and access to catalytic grant finance results in significantly improved short- and long-term success rates.

- Selection and ongoing performance monitoring are key features in the performance of the accelerator.

9

Township Accelerator

Although we don't currently segment township businesses into their own accelerator, they are so important to the small-business ecosystem that no mention of SMME acceleration would be complete without a chapter on township enterprises, and the informal businesses that emerge within them. Rising levels of poverty, under-employment and unemployment in rural areas is spurring major migration into the cities right across the world. The desire to move to safer pastures, with increased opportunity for cross-border and refugee migration, brings with it myriad additional challenges of culture and language, and often hostility towards the incoming migrant.

Where migration of semi-skilled or unskilled workers is out of balance with the rate that the urban economy can absorb them, this leads inevitably to a rapid rise in slum neighbourhoods. In South Africa, cross-border and interprovincial urban migration is resulting in an explosion of new, informal settlements around the cities and increased density of population in the existing townships.

According to the FinScope research, in 2006 an estimated 4,3 million South Africans – 11% of the population – live in informal settlements or townships.[20] And the number continues to grow.[21]

> ## MINI EXPLAINER: Township
>
> The term *township* in South Africa refers to a suburb officially designated under Apartheid for black occupation. Although many decades have passed since the abolition of Apartheid, these suburbs still exist.
>
> Certain townships have now advanced to include areas where wealthy citizens reside, but most are closely associated with disadvantage, poverty and unemployment.
>
> Across the world these townships would be synonymous with informal settlements such as the ghettos of Turkey, the favelas of Brazil and the slums of Ethiopia. All are characterised by common features of poverty, unemployment, lack of infrastructure and municipal services.

The usual viewpoint around urban slums and townships is that they are all bad – and it is indisputable that they are filled with crime, grime and poverty. There is another slant to this, though. They represent a strong signal of future growth, future development and the potential for new shoots of commerce. Investments in infrastructure such as water, roads, sanitation, electricity and housing have the potential to stimulate a local economy from which the secondary small-business community could grow.

Even without this capital investment, it is possible (and vital) to help township residents start and grow successful businesses as a means to escape rampant unemployment and poverty and the related hardships. For this we need a fresh look at viable business models.

Overview of a township accelerator

The township accelerator is a solution crafted to meet the needs of entrepreneurs located in high-density, under-served urban communities. In South Africa attention is placed on supporting black South African citizens, yet there are rising challenges with xenophobia against refugees and against migrants from neighbouring countries.

Accelerators can provide opportunities to build bridges between people from different backgrounds.

The opposite is true when opportunity is segregated into 'them and us'. It's important to consider this when designing or investing in such accelerator programmes.

The problems we are addressing

The township accelerator seeks to tackle a number of problems, as outlined below.

1. Lack of employment opportunities

The problem here is the rapid inward migration of young, often unskilled or semi-skilled individuals to the cities at a rate higher than their absorption into the local jobs market.

2. Living conditions

Urban migrants seek better health care, education, clean water, sanitation and the hope of employment. What they find on arrival are overcrowded, unsafe, informal settlements, many without running water, sanitation, electricity or infrastructure. Violence, especially gender-based violence and gangsterism, is rife.

3. Personal safety

Safety and security are ongoing concerns, and it's increasingly common for successful entrepreneurs to report added dangers in the form of extortion for 'business protection' and even kidnapping of family members in return for ransom.

4. Financial pressures

The additional burden of family expectations can also weigh heavily on the emerging business in which the entrepreneur is expected to care for unemployed and elderly relatives. As you can imagine, with such high unemployment in South Africa, 'black tax' can result in many mouths to feed, putting huge financial and emotional strain on the emerging entrepreneur.

> **MINI EXPLAINER: What is black tax?**
>
> Black tax is a term for financial support that a professional or entrepreneur of colour is obliged to provide to their family on a continuous basis outside of their own living expenses. Sometimes it is taken on subconsciously, as a kind of payback for sacrifices made by previous generations or family members.[22]

These township environments suit agile and informal businesses, of which many thousands exist, some of which are highly successful, with revenues into the millions.[23] Typically, these informal businesses are unregistered, deal in cash, and skirt around the law, which is a risk for the entrepreneur should they want to build the business beyond this stage. Businesses that need capital to grow face a problem as traditional lenders require financial record-keeping and compliance, leaving informal businesses open to the high cost and risks of informal lenders.

5. Market conditions

In South Africa townships are increasingly seen by corporate retailers as an untapped market opportunity, resulting in a rise in the number of shopping malls within townships. This results in their dominance of the local economy, pulling customers away from the smaller stores and businesses and diverting money out of the township economy, further exacerbating the challenges for local small businesses.

The vision for success

The vision for the township accelerator is that entrepreneurs living in slums, townships and ghettos can start and grow successful businesses that provide for their family needs and contribute to economic growth, shared wealth and local job creation amongst the township population.

These township communities represent an opportunity for emerging entrepreneurs. Many of our success stories come from small businesses in the South African townships, where entrepreneurs are close to their client base and understand their customers' needs, wants and buying abilities.

What can go wrong

As you can no doubt imagine, in a township environment many things can go wrong. The pressure of working here can result in mental strain from the relentless pressure of physical and financial insecurity.

This means that the traditional acceleration tools of visibility, branding and brand building need to be carefully applied. Media attention in the press, on radio and on social media is normally a powerful tool for creating visibility for a small business. However, in the township environment this can lead to unwanted attention from gangsters and hijackers; alarmingly, a number of our township entrepreneurs have been victims of this.

Under these circumstances, it's not surprising that many township entrepreneurs prefer to keep a low profile and work under the radar. Whilst this is an understandable strategy, it will limit their growth ambitions or require the entrepreneur to plan a route out of the township by migrating their business and family elsewhere.

Entrepreneurs whose history is built on cash and non-compliance often resist the leap towards formality, and acceleration results can be hampered by this lack of compliance.

In the following case study we look at one of South Africa's most inspiring young entrepreneurs, who has risen from her roots in Katlehong township to create a uniquely African business that has great potential to go far. This truly is a 'township to international stage' success story, showcasing the potential of Africa's unique business talent and personality.

CASE STUDY: Mini township entrepreneur

Jabulile Gwala is the founder of Siko Republik, an athleisure company that merges African prints with active wear. All its fabrics are sourced locally and sublimated with unique prints in its factory in KwaZulu-Natal.

Jabulile describes herself as a Zulu girl, born and bred in Katlehong township, who was inspired by her rich and vibrant Zulu heritage and love for African and Nguni prints, which feature strongly in her designs.

The brand is tailored for African women aged between twenty and forty-five who are looking to celebrate their culture. The company designs and manufactures clothing, and retails to the local and international market. It has grown from a one-man band, operating in a garage, into a thriving, aspirational brand.

Jabulile entered the SAB Foundation Tholoana accelerator with a clear passion. She had a skill for sales and marketing and needed help with the rapidly moving dynamics of her growing business.

During the eighteen-month accelerator programme, Siko Republik was a sell-out success at a runway show. This translated into great exposure for the business as well as a good learning opportunity in understanding the export market. Jabulile was also selected to dress the top ten Miss South Africa finalists.

Investment supplied by the accelerator was channelled into sales and marketing costs, raw materials, and sampling production. The business created thirty-one new jobs and saw rapid increase in revenue as a result of strong, diversified growth.

Following completion of the Tholoana programme, Jabulile has now employed a fashion manager, based in Switzerland, with access to both London and Ghana. Jabulile aims to grow the brand in these markets.

Summary

Townships represent more than just an eyesore on the landscape and more than only the challenges of poverty, lack of infrastructure, and violence. Viewed differently, from an optimistic growth lens, townships represent the bud of possibility, and a growth point waiting to emerge. This dual context – of aspiration to solve the human challenges of economic growth and unemployment, and the desire to unleash the latent talent and innovation that lies within these vibrant communities – makes townships an ideal focus for acceleration.

However, growth strategies in the township must meet the needs of the entrepreneur and their customer, within the hyper-local challenges and norms. For this reason, acceleration needs to be fine-tuned, and the professional team of mentors, coaches and growth partners need to be well attuned to the environment.

Understanding how to work around – or work with – the challenges of violence, crime and cultural barriers becomes essential to successful business growth. This includes an understanding of the resistance entrepreneurs may feel when transitioning from informal to formal business compliance, which is essential to significant expansion.

The mixture of people and problems in townships represents a possibility for fresh, dynamic and innovative business models. I believe that some of the most unique businesses of the future will arise out of these vibrant African communities.

Key takeaways

- Townships and slums are an increasing reality across much of the world, as young people flow towards the cities through cross-border and interprovincial migration.

- Migration is potentially a source of future growth and opportunity, especially where municipal infrastructure is added. However, conditions tend to be extremely harsh, with poor or absent infrastructure and lack of basic amenities, and with overcrowding, violence and poverty.

- Many informal and micro businesses thrive in these communities, providing the seeds for successful small businesses to grow.

- Challenges to growth include risks to safety such as gangsterism and kidnapping, which limits the growth ambitions and possibilities.

- Formalisation and compliance are critical components of scaled growth, which informal township entrepreneurs may resist.

- Development of retail malls in the townships, with their dominance by the large corporate brands, often results in crushing competition for the smaller business. Strategies to counteract this negative effect are important.

10
Post-Disaster Recovery

I'm excited about the success of our post-disaster recovery accelerator, and I am keen to develop a simple, replicable model that can be used elsewhere in the world.

The number of natural disasters has been increasing globally, with a fivefold rise reported between 1970 and 2019. Data shows that this increase is driven by climate change and related extreme weather events.[24] According to the research, the human impact has been felt hardest in developing countries, accounting for more than 91% of disaster-related deaths.

We all felt the effects of the Covid pandemic, which made us very aware just how interconnected we are. Currently, with the conflict in Ukraine and Gaza, we are experiencing how wars and conflict across the globe can affect populations far from the strife.

In an ideal world, disaster recovery is a partnership between local and national governments, civil society, enterprise support organisations (ESOs) such as us, and social investors with the resources to deploy.

Fetola's Post-Disaster Recovery Accelerator model was developed as a recovery strategy for the Covid pandemic. We implemented it in South Africa under the banner of the Circular Economy Accelerator (CEA) Boost programme as a regeneration solution, to help businesses recover from the negative effects of the extensive lockdowns and related economic constraints that placed thousands of small businesses at risk. Although it was designed for this specific situation, it's clear that the methods and lessons we have learnt can be applied in other post-disaster recovery circumstances, and anywhere there is a need to restart a local economy and to help businesses get back on their feet.

Overview of a disaster recovery plan

An organisation's disaster recovery plan (DRP) contains detailed instructions on how the company should respond to unplanned incidents such as natural disasters, power outages and cyberattacks. The DRP includes strategies to minimise the effects of any disaster, enabling the organisation to continue to operate and quickly resume key activities.

The longer the recovery time from disruptions, the more adverse the impact will be on revenue, brand and customer satisfaction. A good DRP therefore enables rapid recovery from any type of disruption.

The problems we are addressing

This accelerator seeks to address a number of problems, including the following.

1. Disasters that create radical changes to the money flow in an economy

This can lead to blockages and constraints, which can crush a small business. Conversely, opportunities for other businesses will be generated, with the potential to explode their growth.

2. Disasters that magnify pre-existing difficulties

An example is market access, which is a persistent problem for emerging businesses in many developing countries, especially those that are transitioning from a closed to a more open economy.

3. Disasters that damage infrastructure

Disruption to roads, water and electricity supply create especially challenging conditions. Those disasters can be the death knell for small businesses already struggling to gain market access. The impact can be widespread, repair takes time, and temporary solutions are costly to apply. This happened after the April 2022 floods in KwaZulu-Natal Province, which caused much devastation and loss of life. The poorer the community and the further it is from the main cities, the longer repair takes and the harder it is hit.

4. Disasters that cause safety and security issues

When law and order break down, small businesses are especially vulnerable to looting and gangsterism, as they seldom have insufficient cash reserves or sufficient insurance to bounce back. The July 2021 riots in KwaZulu-Natal province, for example, had a devastating physical and emotional impact on local communities, from which recovery will take years.

Under such severe pressure, entrepreneurs need specialised help, and they need it fast. They are dealing with major catastrophes and need the right assistance for them to quickly recover, regain stability and return to success. Recovery is further exacerbated where entrepreneurs are traumatised; are frozen with anxiety; or lack the agility, skills and resources to reposition their business.

The effects of disaster on the mental stress and anguish of entrepreneurs and their communities are significant. Emotional support is needed to bolster the entrepreneur's positive mindset and to boost the confidence of the surrounding community.

The Why – vision for success

The vision of the CEA Boost programme was to significantly improve the revenue of businesses struggling in the post-Covid environment. We were determined to deliver a high-impact accelerator that would strengthen existing enterprises, stimulate growth and ensure job security, whilst improving the environmental practices within the enterprise.

We had previously not experienced such a widespread disaster, so this was a new approach to deal with an unusual circumstance. The main hallmarks of this approach are as follows:

- The Boost programme was part of South Africa's first circular economy accelerator, so there was a supporting vision to improve the sustainability and circularity of the businesses alongside their financial recovery.

- Our strategy was to select established small businesses that had the fundamental building blocks of business in place and needed help to regain their footing.

- Our focus was to rescue businesses that had been performing well before the pandemic and were struggling as a result of the disaster, to help them take advantage of the changed circumstances.

- We selected businesses that were deemed recoverable and could deliver a high, positive impact, including job retention and jobs growth.

- The desired outcome was for businesses to regain their financial wellbeing, retain or increase their job count and improve their sustainability footprint through circular economy practices.

Overview of the CEA Boost programme

The CEA Boost programme was launched in 2021 as a post-Covid response. Over a period of six months, it assisted forty-nine entrepreneurs from marginalised communities across the country. Twenty-two (45%) of the candidates were women and twenty-five (51%) were youth-led businesses.

All participants were alumni of a previous growth initiative; eighteen were Fetola alumni, and the remainder came from our partners. There was a focus on environment, circular economy and green-sector businesses. All participants had the basic business foundations in place, although most had fewer than nine staff members.

Businesses were segmented into tiers, according to their needs, and provided with a range of support, including:

- Group mentorship
- Partnership introductions
- 'Go to market' strategies
- Compliance assistance
- Specialist training

Manufacturing businesses also received process re-engineering interventions to reduce waste and improve competitiveness, and some were helped with their applications for concessionary acceleration funding.

For many of the entrepreneurs, *circularity* and *circular economy* (discussed further in the next chapter) were completely new. Training on these concepts helped businesses such as those in the health sector or in furniture manufacture to identify new markets and pivot their model by adopting the circular elements of rental, repair and resale.

This inaugural run of the programme was a success:

- The revenue of the group improved by 22,8% over the six months.

- Entrepreneurs exited the initiative with improved confidence in their future growth.

- There was an increase of 124 new jobs, and 291 jobs were retained.

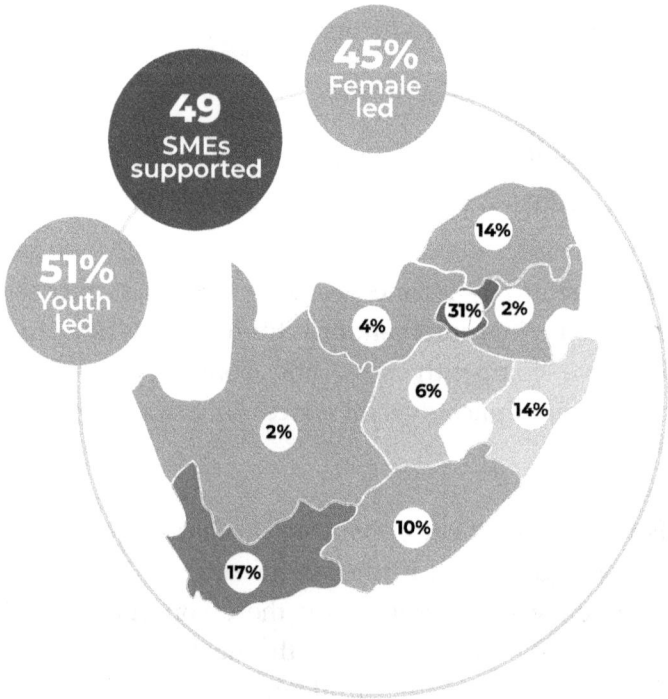

Snapshot of entrepreneurs in the CEA Boost programme

What makes it different?

A few factors made the CEA Boost programme stand out from other accelerators:

- The programme used a *modified* Fetola accelerator model, with discrete, targeted support to stimulate rapid post-disaster recovery.

- The selected enterprises were more established and better suited to the application of a short-term 'boost'. Businesses had the fundamentals of business in place and were actively seeking help for quick recovery. This differs from acceleration of early-stage enterprises, where a longer programme is needed to embed the necessary fundamentals.

- In terms of acceleration, this was a short-term initiative and specifically sought to ensure revenue recovery through targeted market-access assistance.

- Access to recovery finance was supported through associated Covid recovery funds, including government-supported initiatives and partner strategies.

Critical success factors

There are four main critical success factors of a post-recovery initiative such as this, as outlined below.

1. Recovery potential

Careful consideration is needed to select businesses with the potential to recover. In situations such as post-pandemic recovery, there will be hundreds if not thousands of businesses in distress. Ideally, selected businesses should have a positive knock-on effect on others in their value chain and be highly job retentive. This requires a review of their financial position before the disaster and assessment of the net recovery benefit if they survive. Selecting for entrepreneurial resilience is also a critical requirement for success under pressure.

2. Risk evaluation

In the planning stages a risk assessment will identify which factors are within and outside our control, and what can be done to overcome any risk. For example, if floods have destroyed critical infrastructure such as bridges, are there workarounds the entrepreneur can deploy? If not, is support realistically going to result in recovery?

3. Financial assistance

Most small businesses have less than three months of cash reserves, and many even less than this. It's essential to get the money flowing quickly, through improved or diversified access to markets, and through access to recovery finance. Covid funds were on offer during our first run of the programme, although compliance constraints meant that very few businesses secured them.

4. Personal support

As attitude and confidence is critical under stress, the provision of social and psychological support for entrepreneurs – in the form of peer groups, coaching and access to mental health practitioners – can be a game changer.

What can go wrong

In a high-pressure post-disaster situation, the need to move swiftly and effectively can be the difference between success and failure of the business, with lasting consequences for stakeholders. As always, things can go wrong.

A focused quick-wins acceleration programme has great appeal, with both the entrepreneur and investor wanting immediate impact. However, careful planning is needed to ensure that results 'stick' and successes don't fade away as quickly as they come. The main challenges to be overcome are described below.

1. Expectations

In high-pressure situations, unrealistic expectations need to be managed. Quick wins can be difficult to deliver, and fast-tracking a business to success is not always possible. Growth that is built consistently over time is often more sustainable than force-fed

151

results, but here the focus is on urgent recovery. In a post-disaster environment, external mitigating factors may make recovery very difficult. These factors include the compromised personal circumstances of the entrepreneur, for example, ill health, loss of premises, or family trauma.

Mismatched expectations can also arise when the entrepreneur overstates their readiness for rapid growth, perhaps not realising the extent of their internal challenges such as poor product quality, production consistency or financial management. Similarly, in seeking a quick market-access solution, the programme might mistakenly assess the business as a good match to a commercial market – perhaps the entrepreneur has no appetite for the restrictive administration requirements of large-scale supply chains, or perhaps logistical constraints mean that volume of production cannot be met.

Upfront decisions are needed on whether this is a business rescue or business boost initiative. Commonly, entrepreneurs asking for support are in some state of challenge. They may want to take advantage of new opportunities and need help with systems, skills shortages and cash flow; or they might be in distress and floundering under challenges of weak revenue flow and excessive overheads. Business rescue requires more extensive support, and challenges are unlikely to be resolved in a six-month, quick-win initiative.

2. Market access

Broad-scale market access requires a team that is well networked and appraised of current market demands and trends. Where economies have broken down, a focus on stimulating local business to business ecosystems is needed. More ambitious regional or export-orientated programmes may require specialist technical support that cannot be concluded in a tight timeline.

3. Communication

In remote locations and in circumstances where electricity and communications infrastructure has been disrupted, low-data, low-hassle communication methods are needed for maintaining rapport, providing assistance, and gathering accurate information and data. These methods have to meet the technology and access realities of the entrepreneurs.

4. Corruption

Corruption is a significant challenge in many African countries. According to the Transparency International Corruption Perception Index 2021, Sub-Saharan Africa remains the region with the highest levels of corruption globally, with a score of 32 out of 100, below the global average of 43.[25] Sadly, corruption and gangsterism often go hand in hand with disastrous situations, so awareness of this and support for entrepreneurs is important.

5. Economic environment

The post-disaster economy is exactly that: a disaster-stricken economy, which needs to recover. Problems will run deeper than the struggles of any individual business, and a simplistic approach to such a challenge risks falling short if it fails to identify and address fundamental changes in the surrounding eco-system. The post-Covid world completely disrupted traditional work routines, introducing home-based work, internet shopping and altered relationships with health and wellbeing. An initiative such as the CEA Boost programme can help entrepreneurs iden-tify and capitalise on these changing trends.

CASE STUDY: Trudy Mkansi

The case of Trudy Mkansi is an interesting one. She joined the CEA Boost programme seeking post-Covid support to restart her furniture business. Severe lockdown restrictions had impacted the business, sales were down, and she had the responsibility of paying salaries to many employees.

Through the new insights gained from circular economy training, and encouragement to search for Covid-related disruptions to exploit, she succeeded in finding new ways to do business.

With summer coming, and with disruptions in international shipping, which resulted in short supply of imported Chinese cane furniture, local importers approached Trudy for help in resolving their stock shortages. In the process, she realised two important points:

1. She embraced the new concept of circularity by introducing a repair service to the business, which brought in immediate cash flow through a contract to repair imported and poorer quality furniture. Now, if a client needs persuading, a visit to Trudy's factory is a visual and tactile guide to the differences in quality between the cheap imports in repair and the quality product she manufactures.

2. She learnt that, in relation to the imported furniture, her range was overengineered and outside the competitive price point. This gave birth to the dream to develop a luxury range, focusing on the superior quality, lifetime guarantee and high value of customised, locally made furniture.

Trudy saw encouraging growth on the CEA Boost programme. Whilst revenue showed a steady increase, the company's most remarkable achievement was in job creation, with an amazing 23,08% increase in employees.

This growth not only reflects positively on Ambesha Africa's expanding workforce, but it also underscores the company's commitment to community development and economic empowerment.

The CEA Boost programme gave Trudy renewed self-confidence and the enthusiasm to build agility into her business model. She was able to kickstart her cash flow through repairs and, with the development of a new luxury range, catapult her business into a new age.

Summary

The evidence is that, with the increasing impact of climate change and rising numbers of natural disasters across the globe, the need for disaster recovery solutions is set to rise. As investors in the future of small business, we need to do two things:

1. Help businesses to be more resilient and pre-empt the impact of possible disasters

2. Be prepared, as the recovery support teams with the right skills and resources, to respond quickly to kickstart the affected economies

Short-term acceleration initiatives that are well-designed and implemented have the potential to stimulate recovery and create quick wins. Solutions such as our post-disaster recovery CEA Boost model can deliver high-impact results. These results help to re-establish struggling enterprises by stimulating revenue, retaining jobs, and helping enterprises to pivot and take advantage of changed markets.

In practice, though, the fragility of businesses in a post-disaster situation, and the changed and dynamic environment in which they now operate, requires the highest level of support skills available. Skilled professions are needed to identify and meet individual business needs, providing the right advice and support to implement agile, future-focused solutions.

In addition, the social and behavioural skills of coaching and change management are needed to calm the nerves, temper the fears, and support the ambitions of the entrepreneur to ensure that the business manages this new situation.

In these rapidly changing environments, the ability to meet the needs of each entrepreneur becomes important. Whilst a simple formula for success provides the guide rails, the programme leadership and methods need to be agile, practical and implementable. Entrepreneur selection, rigorous business and market gap analysis, access to growth capital, and clear timelines need to be managed to deliver the best outcomes.

With the CEA Boost programme, sustainability thinking and circular economy practices significantly improved the entrepreneurs' ability to rethink their product–market fit and open up fresh recovery opportunities.

Key takeaways

1. Solutions for post-disaster recovery that help entrepreneurs get back on their feet can enable local economies to regenerate.

2. Focused solutions are applied to businesses that have the potential to recover or to pivot into new opportunities generated by the disaster.

3. Consideration needs to be given to the resilience of the entrepreneur, whether the business is recoverable, and the wider community impact of the business's success or failure.

4. Quick wins with access to markets, workarounds where infrastructure has been damaged, and access to recovery finance are important.

5. Care for the mental health of entrepreneurs under such strain needs consideration.

6. The addition of circular-economy training and awareness results in significant changes to the way of doing business and opens new markets with additional revenue benefits.

11

Sector-Specific Accelerator

I have chosen to use the circular economy as the focus area in this sector-specific accelerator model, as I am passionate about circular economy thinking. It makes perfect environmental and business sense. Coming from a small town in Zambia, where I spent many hours in the bush, on the farm and travelling through the countryside for work and study, I have seen firsthand how quickly environmental devastation happens. Hills that were once covered in natural woodland are now denuded and bare; rivers that were pristine are poisoned and toxic.

Despite decades of information about better practices, farmers still scrape the land; burn the residues; use chemical fertiliser, herbicides and pesticides. The degradation has happened slowly, inch by inch. We now find ourselves surrounded by a global catastrophe, with worsening air and water pollution impacting the health of all the planet's peoples.

There is another way, though. This chapter's case study showcases how small changes in the behaviour of businesses can alter the planet's disastrous trajectory.

Some accelerators focus on discrete challenges – such as gender, age or sector-specific enterprises – to achieve a single aim. Segmentation like this reduces implementation complexity and can appeal to partners whose own strategy corresponds to the specific challenge. This focus can also make it easier to attract technical and market support from industry. Common sector-focus areas include:

- Technology
- Health
- Mining
- Agriculture

In this chapter we will focus on sustainability, with our lens on the circular economy.

The circular economy is gaining attention in South Africa as a promising lever to stimulate healthy growth. A 2021 study by the Council for Scientific and Industrial Research champions the case for circularity as a way in which the highly extractive, carbon-intensive, wasteful and water-scarce South African economy can be transformed to one that is better for its social and environmental health.[26]

One of the delights of the Fetola Circular Economy Accelerator (CEA) is its mixture of entrepreneurs, reflecting the full demographics of society. This richness allows for the vibrant, cross-cultural interplay that encourages innovation. This kind of integration is unusual in South Africa today, where BBBEE laws create walls between entrepreneurs of different ethnic backgrounds. However, how can a dynamic business partnership between a white Afrikaans professor from Bloemfontein and a young black engineer from the Eastern Cape emerge unless they have the chance to meet and work together? Entrepreneurship is a wonderful way to build a united future, and I would like to see mixed accelerators happen more often.

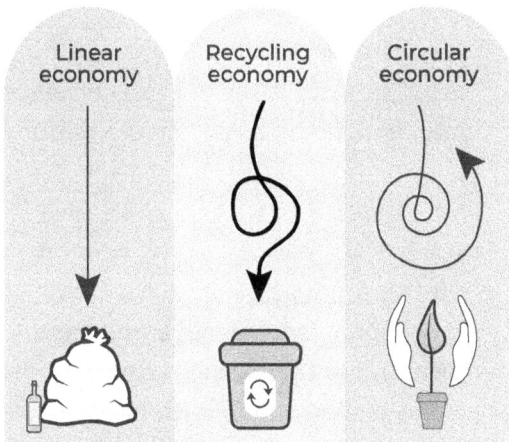

Circularity explainer

> **MINI EXPLAINER: The circular economy**
>
> The term *circular economy* is used to describe a life-cycle process in which waste is designed out of the system, enabling all the components in the production and consumption process to remain in use. Nothing goes to waste. It goes beyond the concept of waste recycling to include sharing, leasing, reusing, repairing and refurbishing of materials and products. It is a practical way to reduce impact on the climate, reduce carbon production, and retain the biodiversity and health of the environment.
>
> To understand more about the many different models for the circular economy, a good go-to resource for simple and practical information is the Ellen MacArthur Foundation.[27]

The problems we are addressing

The CEA model goes beyond simply helping businesses to grow in size. It seeks to foster enterprises that will make a lasting, positive environmental impact.

South Africa has an old-fashioned economy, using very high levels of fossil fuel for energy creation and transportation. Traditionally, the country has depended heavily on the extractive mining industry. Agriculture too is old-school, with heavy use of artificial fertilisers and chemicals. Historically, economic actors have shown little regard for the environment and had very few formal incentives to change their attitudes towards the environment.

This approach is out of sync with other parts of the world, where sustainability is becoming a major concern for citizens, businesses and their governments. Most countries now acknowledge that the effects of global warming are accelerating at an alarming rate. The evidence is especially obvious in increasingly extreme weather patterns. Consequently, the drive to slow down climate change (mitigation) and to manage its now inevitable impact (adaptation) is a discussion point in leading corporate boardrooms throughout the developed world.

In much of the developing world, and in South Africa particularly, more immediate problems – including mass unemployment, inequality and abject poverty – make global warming and environmental sustainability seem less pressing concerns.

Our challenge is to create enterprises with clear market appeal that are environmentally positive, profitable and socially acceptable. In Africa, where the population is growing rapidly, job creation is also a key component of any successful business model.

Being 'first to market' with new ideas, such as the concept of circular economy thinking in South Africa, adds a layer of expense to the development of a business, in the form of advocacy, the cost of which can be considerable. Small businesses often miscalculate the time and resources needed for advocacy campaigns to educate and attract customers to their new ideas or products. Over the years, we have seen lots of entrepreneurial passion for building sustainability products and services but a reluctance on the part of customers, especially larger organisations, to switch to them.

The Why – vision for success

Fetola's vision for the Circular Economy Accelerator was to build a cohort of thriving circular economy businesses that are financially sound and create meaningful jobs, whilst also having a positive impact on the environment. Each success should create a slipstream for others to follow, through open engagement with stakeholders and sharing of knowledge. Each CEA blends pure business acceleration with the goal of transitioning businesses from the old patterns of wasteful linear thinking to circular economy production and consumption models.

By 2024 the need for environmentally sound business practices should be clear to all. The reality, though, is that entrenched profit-making mindsets within the fossil-fuel industry and related value chain are still resistant to these changes. Instead of waiting for miraculous agreement at government and corporate level, our task as business growth specialists is to make these changes happen from the ground up – one small business, one entrepreneur at a time. In this way we can make a difference across the entire small-business ecosystem.

From my perspective, circularity finally provides a sustainability model that makes business sense. It is easy to explain and understand. This is exciting! Circularity overcomes past challenges, where sustainability was viewed as an unnecessary luxury. In short, sustainability was considered a 'bunny hugger's' solution that had no place in a serious business value chain. In contrast, the circular economy model is easier to motivate in business circles, because a model that drives out waste is appealing and easily understood. As the climate change agenda rapidly rises in importance with punitive taxes on imports, circularity will receive increasingly favourable corporate response, even in a country such as South Africa.

As many circular economy business models are labour-absorbing and have low barriers to entry – such as those that reuse, repair and repurpose – circularity is a viable solution in developing nations with large job-seeking populations.

Overview of the Circular Economy Accelerator

Fetola's CEA was the first such entity in South Africa. The programme we created was an eighteen-month accelerator, targeting small businesses, with a plan to embrace a circular economy model as a profitable way to:

- Reduce costs

- Decrease climate impact

- Improve environmental impact

Meanwhile, our additional purpose was to support job growth and sustainable profitability in our small-business clients.

Our CEA used all elements of the Fetola Growth Method.

Target enterprises were chosen from marginalised areas from all corners of South Africa. We included townships and urban and rural areas, which offered the greatest potential to impact livelihoods through increased employment, inclusive wealth and environmentally sound practices. Here are some of the positive outcomes:

- Our CEA provided a transformational growth journey to a national cohort of businesses, empowering entrepreneurs to build thriving, profitable and environmentally sustainable small businesses.

- Our programme left a lasting legacy, in strengthening leadership skills and building entrepreneurial self-confidence. They received technical skills, business skills training and sector knowledge; gained access to opportunities for collaboration and growth; built their brands, networks and client bases; and increased their ability to access markets and growth finance.

- Our methods helped candidates refine their business models and adopt circular elements which opened up new revenue streams and improved profitability.

The CEA programme has been immensely successful. All the forty-six entrepreneurs that graduated from the accelerator rated it 10 out of 10. Positive results were achieved across all the target measures, with all businesses adding to and improving their circularity. This resulted in significant increases in revenue, doubling of profitability levels and the addition of new jobs.

What makes it different?

The overriding distinguishing feature of Fetola's CEA model is the targeted intention to support circularity. As this is a new concept in South Africa, the accelerator started with circular economy training for the participants, the project team and the business mentors. This training was carefully crafted for the target audience and focused on practical understanding rather than highly theoretical concepts and models, which so often dominate this field.

Other points that make our CEA different from other accelerator programmes include:

- As circularity is a global movement, built on collaboration and sharing of ideas, the accelerator easily accessed assistance from global networks. The CEA advisory panel was drawn from across the world, bringing diverse experience into the design and implementation of the programme.

- Circularity differs from traditional business models that centre on protection of individual intellectual property. With collaborative methods and sharing platforms, circular businesses change this old style of thinking to create a *sharing* ethos.

- The accelerator played an important advocacy and awareness role within the SMME ecosystem, as we tapped into global knowledge and advocacy support networks. This helped to reduce the cost of advocacy.

- Investors tend to view sustainability businesses as high risk, making access to finance even more difficult. Fetola was successful in establishing a special green finance grant fund, which will be used to prove and expand access to finance for green businesses.

Group picture from the workshop

What can go wrong

As with any accelerator, we needed to consider potential risks. Those related to the sector-specific CEA, are outlined below.

1. Impact measurement

One of the biggest unresolved challenges we faced was identifying impact measurement tools suitable for small circular businesses.

Environmental impact data is vital currency. Data that proves the business is doing what it claims to be doing forms an unshakeable platform of support for the brand. Supporting data differentiates the business, yet the complexity of the circularity model makes meaningful measurement of data difficult. Many entrepreneurs struggled with this.

Without simple monitoring tools, data is either not collected, or it is fictitious and does not stand up to scrutiny. Further work is needed to develop monitoring tools that are suitable for this purpose.

2. Selection

For this accelerator, entrepreneur selection was a particular challenge. Given that circularity was a new concept in South Africa, few applicants had heard of it, and even fewer met the circular business criteria. We therefore needed to adjust and pivot the programme to accommodate this.

Our goal was for sixty-five businesses. Even with our new adjustments, we could only select forty-nine participants that met the criteria. Three of these dropped out over the eighteen months.

3. Group think

Group think is one of the potential downsides of tight focus in an accelerator. Entrepreneurs who are all similar (same sector, gender, stage of business, etc) can easily slip into a fixed, closed mindset. The group may assume a problem to be intractable and 'just how it is', where a more heterogeneous mindset would challenge this automatic assumption.

Evidence supports the value of diversity in problem solving, where the inclusion of non-specialists often results in faster, more agile problem solving. As Adam Grant outlines in his book *Think Again,* diversity increases the possibilities for innovation.[28]

Uniform groups also limit out-of-sector collaboration, which is such a useful feature of mixed acceleration cohorts.

4. Greenwashing

Lasting changes in sustainability require a lifetime commitment, not a quick greenwashing. Accelerator programmes therefore need to ensure they are making genuine strides to build small suppliers who are ambassadors for the planet.

In South Africa, where unemployment is reaching towards the 40% mark and economic growth is below 1%, unlike in many parts of Europe, the national priority is jobs, not environmental sustainability.[29] Programmes in the sustainability sector therefore require strong industry networks, to identify and engage corporations committed to environmental change, with strong advocacy to expand into additional markets.

5. Technical expertise

Sector-specific accelerators imply a focus on specific technical expertise; however, technical expertise alone is not enough. A balanced support of core business skills – 'the business of business' – plus technical skills are required.

A common mistake is to concentrate solely on technical expertise, resulting in a business model that never gains traction.

6. Finance

Entrepreneurs with highly innovative ideas need to be realistic about access to finance. Businesses with a deep and wide 'valley of death' between concept and profitability are unlikely to survive without significant investment. It is difficult for small businesses to obtain investment at the best of times, and it can be even harder where investors perceive additional risk in unproven markets.

Partnering with a supportive investment fund and providing entrepreneurs with strong investment readiness support can help to unlock growth finance.

Examples of circularity entrepreneurs

A wide range of inspiring entrepreneurs participated in the CEA. These included businesses that already had a well-developed circularity focus. One example is Jami Nash from EC Waste Management, a specialist electronics waste management company in KwaZulu-Natal. Another example is Joel van der Schyff of AgriLogiq, which provides technology solutions to farmers that help them reduce their energy, water and chemical usage, whilst raising crop productivity, thereby improving profitability and significantly reducing the environmental impact of greenhouses.

Entrepreneurs that pivoted into circularity include Natasha Pearce of Vivacious Eco Vixon, winner of the CEA graduate award. Natasha refocused her gifting business to make it entirely sustainability-driven, eliminating waste throughout the business and tapping into the growing sustainability interest from corporate South Africa.

On the opposite end of the spectrum is Zenzile Silvia Mabitsela, who initially raised and sold live chickens from her smallholding in a township outside Johannesburg. Zenzile was unaware of the circular economy before joining the CEA. Now her company, Masana Generation Project, sells chicken manure to local farmers, thereby supporting the circular economy practice of regenerative farming.

The following case study features an entrepreneur from the construction sector. It illustrates how changes can be made at small-business level, even in a traditionally highly carbon-emitting and environmentally destructive industry.

CASE STUDY: Circular economy

Sihle Lindiwe Vilakazi is a young entrepreneur on a mission to change the way that people view construction. After a career in tourism and nine years working in the Government Parks and Recreation Department, she decided to branch out and start her own company, Kelo Group. Her big vision is to develop urban 'Afri-villages' that give residents the opportunity to live in green, sustainable buildings. These foster sustainable communities in the city, ensuring a circular economic environment, where each community is off-grid and can produce their own food, selling off surplus produce and raising kids who understand the importance of food gardens and green buildings.

Most eco-sensitive developers are looking only to build green. They are not striving also to continue the sustainable living offering by building communities that can successfully function in a circular economic way. Lindiwe believes that eco estates of the future should include a healthy mix of income levels, and that gardens of the future should be used to grow food rather than being only ornamental beautification.

Already a circular economy fan, Lindiwe joined CEA needing help to focus on her business fundamentals such as financial record keeping, niche-market differentiation, and business systems and processes.

Despite the challenges of being a black woman in the construction industry, with the help of the accelerator team during the eighteen months of the programme, Kelo Group grew its revenue by 339% in turnover and secured a large building project in Randburg, Johannesburg. With her new investment readiness skills, Lindiwe also made successful applications for growth finance.

After entering the accelerator as a one-woman band, Kelo Group now employs seventeen people. Lindiwe wisely chose to grow the business in the 'circular way' by also building a network of partners and contractors. As one job in South Africa supports on average 3,4 dependants, these seventeen jobs translate to direct benefit for an additional fifty-eight people.

Summary

Sector-specific accelerators have appeal for their uniformity and their ability to apply seamless, focused solutions. The commonality of technical, market and supply chain challenges can enable a simpler accelerator model, thereby reducing complexity and the cost of implementation. However, this focus is not without its downsides. Careful attention may be needed to avoid group think by fostering ways to encourage out-of-sector cross-collaboration and innovation.

As the world deals with looming environmental disasters posed by climate change, and industry and country policies develop to match, there will be a greater need for accelerators that incorporate circular economy models. Sound, professional methods into the building of profitable businesses that are good for people and the planet will also be needed.

Access to finance remains a concern for the growing business, and more solutions for this are needed. Whilst sector focus can be helpful in identifying investors with the same end goal and building intimate knowledge of how to develop a compelling investment case, this remains a challenge for sustainability businesses, which are deemed high risk by most investors.

In Fetola we are excited about the catalytic investment solutions that have arisen from this accelerator, and by our new pilot green grant fund, dedicated to sustainable small businesses. Working with our partners, we hope to further prove the viability of these innovative finance solutions at scale so that we can support the success of many thousands of profitable, people- and planet-friendly businesses.

Key takeaways

- The circular economy is a powerful tool in ensuring business and environmental benefit.

- Single-sector focus accelerators are attractive to many partners, as they are less complex to implement and can attract partners with the same focus.

- Marketing to a uniform audience is easier, but if the tight focus results in few applicants, there is a danger that cohort size and quality are affected.

- Where challenges arise, accelerators and partners need to be open to pivoting and adjusting their strategies.

- Access to finance for sustainability businesses is difficult, requiring patient partnerships and trust building to reduce perceived risk.

- Peer-group engagement, sharing and collaboration can have immense positive effects on the confidence and success of the businesses.

12
Social Enterprise Accelerator

I often tell people that my day job is creating jobs, but what keeps me awake at night is pondering how to create meaning for the many millions of South Africans, especially young South Africans, who are increasingly unlikely to ever find paid employment. This depressing prospect is true for many regions of the world.

We work enthusiastically to build small businesses that will grow the economy, create inclusive wealth and generate jobs, but we must not neglect the other, much larger side of society that also desperately needs our help. This is the domain of the social enterprise, where committed, socially minded leaders build profitable businesses, designed to have a positive social impact. Social entrepreneurship sits between the for-profit business and charity or non-profit enterprises. The Social Enterprise model is more difficult to perfect, as it requires a balance between the profit motive and the desire to assist the less fortunate. In addition, we now understand that to serve our fellow earthlings, the social enterprise must be environmentally sound – a business that degrades the environment in which it operates will have a net negative impact on society. As the CEO of Walmart, Doug McMillon, said succinctly in his interview with Simon Sinek, 'You can't have profit if you don't have a planet.'[30]

Overview of a social enterprise

Formal definitions differ. The law in South Africa does not yet recognise the social enterprise as a formal business registration. Certain jurisdictions already recognise businesses, as Certified B Corporations, meeting high standards of verified performance, accountability and transparency, on factors from supply chain practices to employee benefits and charitable giving. It will be up to South Africa's legal scholars to formulate legislation that will allow social enterprises to operate within and benefit from a dedicated social enterprise law.

Social enterprises seek to earn profits, but their primary goal is to serve a public mission. Their social mission is their raison d'être.

MINI EXPLAINER: The social enterprise

The concept of social enterprise is rapidly evolving in practice and in theory. Eventually, the law will catch up with practices developed by real-world participants in this new sector of the economy. For the time being, we can say that a social enterprise is a business that combines the profit motive with one or more clearly defined social objectives:

- Unlike traditional business, profit is not the sole goal of a social enterprise.

- Unlike typical for-profit businesses, which may produce incidental social benefits such as charitable contributions, the social mission is the central raison d'être of a social enterprise.

- Unlike a charity, social enterprises generate revenue by selling goods and services to fund their social mission.

- Unlike a nonprofit, the owners of a social enterprise expect, and are entitled to, a monetary return on their investment.

- Unlike charities and nonprofit corporations, social enterprises may attract investment capital.

- Generally, employment preference is given to people from at-risk communities.

Overview of the Social Enterprise Impact Lab SEIL

The Social Enterprise Impact Lab (SEIL) is an example of Fetola's social enterprise accelerator model in action. SEIL is designed to alleviate the challenges faced by marginalised South African communities by enhancing the sustainability and investment readiness of social enterprises. Important factors include:

- The eighteen-month accelerator follows the full Fetola Growth Method, with a strong focus on improved financial wellbeing, to enable the enterprise to access much-needed growth capital.

- Social enterprises are selected for their strong social mandate and potential to generate significant social impact in marginalised communities.

- The accelerator focuses on supporting the overall healthy growth of the social enterprise through a first phase of business consolidation. The second phase concentrates on improving financial readiness, with the goal of matching investment in individual enterprises with the immediate potential to scale.

- The social enterprises selected to participate in the programme include a wide diversity of businesses from across the country, which target a range of sustainable development goals (SDGs).

MINI EXPLAINER: What is an SDG?

SDGs were adopted by the United Nations in 2015 as a universal call to action to end poverty, protect the planet and ensure that by 2030 all people enjoy peace and prosperity.

These goals remind us that development must balance social, economic and environmental sustainability, and that action in one area affects outcomes in others.[31]

Exceptional results have been obtained by the social enterprises Fetola selected to participate in our most recent programme. The 29 social enterprises that graduated in 2023 showed a 46% revenue growth and created 65 new jobs. These enterprises also used their strengthened investment readiness to access significant amounts of development finance, which is so critical for their continued growth. Of the investment-ready enterprises, 75% successfully raised catalytic growth finance, an astounding success given the financing challenges so dominant in the sector.

The enterprises collectively reported impact on specific SDGs as follows:

- SDG 2: Zero hunger
- SDG 3: Good health and wellbeing
- SDG 4: Quality education
- SDG 6: Clean water and sanitation

- SDG 12: Responsible consumption and production

- SDG 15: Life on land

Previous cohorts focused on the SDGs:

- SDG 1: No poverty

- SDG 8: Decent work and economic growth

- SDG 3: Good health and wellbeing

The problems we are addressing

The overarching problem for the social enterprise accelerator is in how to craft business-like solutions that solve persistent social and environmental challenges, including those described below.

1. Unemployment

The developing world faces a stark social problem of mass unemployment. Figures from the JobsNowAfrica Coalition show that ten million to twelve million African youth enter the workforce each year, yet only three million formal jobs are created.[32]

That leaves seven to nine million young people excluded from the workforce every single year. With each year adding another cohort of young people to this vast army of unemployed talent, the possibility of their eventual gainful employment recedes. They have not been picked for the team, and they may never be picked for the team. Inevitably, many of these disappointed youths turn to crime, dissipation or illegal emigration.

2. Education

Lack of education is intrinsically connected to this problem of mass unemployment. The future of any country rests on the quality of its education, and South Africa owes her young citizens access to an education that is relevant for their needs. Whilst primary education and literacy rates have improved since Apartheid, there are still considerable gaps in quality, particularly in secondary and higher education.

Very few secondary schools have computers, and even fewer have science laboratories. Science, technology, engineering and maths, which make up STEM, are essential tools for employment, yet only 6% of South African school leavers are achieving the university grade pass rate of 60% for maths.[33] This shocking statistic represents a national disaster in the making.

3. Health services

Many African nations continue to face significant challenges in providing accessible, high-quality health care. Key issues include infrastructure, a shortage of trained health care professionals, and limited access to essential medicines and medical technologies. The prevalence of infectious diseases such as HIV/AIDS and malaria further strains Africa's already overburdened health care systems.

A pervasive sense of hopelessness, and the loss of dignity that comes with poverty and joblessness, means that mental health services are essential. Cultural stigma around mental health, and a lack of mental health support add to the problem.

4. Gender-based violence and child abuse

Gender-based violence (GBV) continues to be a widespread problem, affecting millions of women and girls. According to the United Nations, one in three women worldwide will experience GBV in their lifetime, and women in the developing world are particularly vulnerable due to entrenched gender inequality, poverty, and lack of access to education and health care.[34]

GBV is further fuelled by a breakdown of strong family bonds, resulting from urban migration and ghetto living.

In summary, there is no shortage of social challenges for the budding social enterprise to address. Solving these complex problems at scale requires the active engagement of the government. In many developing countries, though, the government is unable or unwilling to help or mismatched to the agile partnerships that are needed to solve these challenges.

The Why – vision for success

The 'Why' for the social enterprise accelerator is so powerful, it almost feels unnecessary to spell it out, but not all citizens are in touch with the importance of social impact. The motivation for social enterprise is the desire to create a society in which all citizens can live a life of dignity, freedom and purpose. Realising this vision requires every person to be given access to education, health care, housing, water and sanitation. If these basic human needs can be met for everyone, everyone will be free to realise their full potential.

Completely capitalist economies are supposed to maximise profit for the shareholders and view social impact as either a distraction from their main purpose or inevitable collateral damage. In reality, capitalists as diverse as Henry Ford, Andrew Carnegie and the Cadbury Brothers have long recognised that the welfare of their workers has a direct bearing on the success of their business.

The Covid pandemic proved, if nothing else, that no man is an island. The lack of a reliable universal health system harms everyone in the society; even if a few are able to seclude themselves in their gated mansions, their fortunes will be affected by the economic impact of mass disease and the corresponding social upheaval. Unless you are invested in the security sector, social upheaval is not good for business.

The vision for the social enterprise accelerator is to create an ecosystem of viable, financially sustainable enterprises that help to solve some of the most pressing needs and deliver tangible social and environmental benefits.

What makes it different?

The social enterprise accelerator is unique in that it focuses exclusively on supporting the social enterprise entities. This focus leads to additional differentiating aspects, for example:

- The socially minded tendencies of social entrepreneurs means that their needs – both psychological and technical – differ from 'regular' small-business founders. Mentors and coaches with experience in social enterprise are needed to navigate this world, guiding founders in the journey to profitable social enterprises.

- The accelerator training content is aligned to social enterprise revenue models, appropriate sales and marketing methods, and financial guidance.

- As social enterprises may require governmental or corporate partnerships to deliver their impact, the ability of an accelerator to foster these partnerships is important. For example, for a health-tech or ed-tech solution to deeply impact the ecosystem, they will need to work alongside Government Departments of Health or Education. Formulating these partnerships can be frustratingly slow, adding significant time and resource costs to the growth journey. The ability to fast-track relationships or build workaround solutions will make or break a success outcome.

- Since social enterprises need to monitor and report on their second currency – their social and environmental impact – training and individual support in compiling and analysing relevant data is provided. As we understand how partners in the governmental and private sectors measure these non-financial outcomes, we identify which impact measures to use and educate social entrepreneurs accordingly. It's important to reduce the complexity of data collection and simplify the measurement and verification of these measures.

- Possibly most challenging, the accelerator needs to provide appropriate investment readiness that leads to access to growth finance. Social enterprise models often require significant amounts of early-stage and start-up finance to bridge the valley of death between concept and profitability, meaning that the ability to improve their investment potential is a critical success factor.

What can go wrong

As you will have gathered by now, social enterprise acceleration is more challenging than standard business acceleration. There are therefore increased possibilities for things to go wrong, as detailed below.

1. Profit-conscious model

The fundamental starting point for a successful social enterprise must be a viable revenue model. This requires a profit-motivated, energetic belief system to drive it, yet many socially minded founders struggle with the concept. A mindset that is subconsciously opposed to profit-making can block progress of the social enterprise.

2. A viable revenue model

These societal challenges demand solutions delivered to people in underserved, poverty-ridden communities, where purchasing power is limited. This lack of resources, infrastructure and income may mean that, despite the need, social enterprises attempting to build a business simply cannot establish a viable revenue model. In such cases the venture is better suited to the charity or non-profit sector rather than to a social enterprise.

3. Stakeholder expectations

Given the unique nature of the social enterprise accelerator model, it's important to align partners and participants. Participants who misunderstand the difference between a self-sustaining social enterprise and a non-profit-funded model can become frustrated when the accelerator doesn't meet their expectations. Similarly, other stakeholders can misunderstand social enterprise, believing it to be simply a commercial business model with a slight twist, not recognising the importance of social return on investment over pure revenue growth.

4. Financial requirements

Many social enterprises are slow to build, with a long and fragile runway to success. Revenue models that are built on high numbers and low profit margins can take years to reach viability. Understanding and matching the financial need of the social enterprise to the accelerator offering is vital. More simply put: if the enterprise needs five years and R1 million grant funding to break even, and the accelerator is eighteen months in duration with R100 000, then it's not a match!

5. Impact measurement

Impact measurement is a bugbear for most small businesses. For social enterprises these measurements are their lifeblood, so education around the SDGs, assistance to identify what and how to measure, and why and how to report impact data is needed.

6. Outside assistance

Government support is critical to the successful scaling of many social enterprises, yet this can be a challenge, especially when the social problem is a result of weak or ineffectual government in the first place. If the government is corrupt, inefficient, or lacks the willingness to branch out and test fresh ideas, growth at scale may be very difficult. Where this is a problem, the ability to develop workarounds such as corporate–citizen collaborations is key.

> **MINI ENTREPRENEUR CASE STUDY: Zinacare**
>
> When Philip Mngadi entered the Social Enterprise Impact Lab Accelerator (SEIL) with his embryo social enterprise, Zinacare, his primary focus was to improve ease of access to medical testing and screening in the sexual health and women's health markets.
>
> At the onset of the Covid outbreaks, Zinacare found themselves positioned to respond, and they rapidly pivoted to establish drive-thru Covid testing facilities

in Gauteng. The drive-thru provided people with convenient access to Covid testing, with results provided within forty-eight hours.

The problem that Philip experienced was managing the rapid scale-up of the business, which required access to additional cash flow facilities and improved financial management.

With strong wraparound support from the SEIL, Zinacare made rapid growth during lockdown, launching a number of drive-thrus, and an on-demand testing service for company employees. With focused investment readiness support to help improve their investment pitch decks, the business managed to secure additional grant finance before exiting the programme. Employment numbers increased 600% in this period, as more staff were needed at each testing point.

The foundational support of the SEIL enabled Zinacare to access further growth finance and scale-up support from a suite of investors after completion of the programme.

Zinacare reports their impact in four of the SDGs, namely:

- SDG 3: Good health and wellbeing
- SDG 8: Decent work and economic growth
- SDG 9 : Build resilient infrastructure, promote sustainable industrialization and foster innovation.
- SDG 11: Make cities and human settlements inclusive, safe, resilient and sustainable

The company is on the road to becoming a thriving social enterprise with a viable revenue model and making a lasting impact on people with health needs.

Summary

Social enterprises play an important role in a world where millions live in impoverished communities. Although global levels of poverty have improved, the number of people living in poverty in Africa is increasing, which puts a strong focus on social impact solutions for this continent.

Rapidly advancing technology developments such as AI – in the form of ChatGPT and other easily accessible tools – will enable social enterprises to deliver more efficient, cost-effective and accessible services in areas such as health care, education and finance. However, such technology is also likely to exacerbate inequality by replacing low-skilled jobs, widening the gap between the rich and the poor, and further cementing the existing digital divide.

By working together in corporate and government partnerships, and across countries, we can nurture social enterprises that serve the trio of people, planet and profitability.

Key takeaways

- Social enterprise is a uniquely different business model that uses self-supporting revenue models to provide much-needed social impact.

- Social enterprise models that require large numbers with low-profit margins face a long, slow climb to profitability. Access to early-growth finance can be very difficult to obtain, leading to early failure in many social enterprises.

- Clear communication between stakeholders is needed to ensure that participants and partners are aligned on the purpose and focus of the social enterprise accelerator, in which social impact – not profit – is the main intention.

- Multilevel partnerships between social enterprises and government are often needed to build impact at scale, yet they can be difficult and time-consuming to achieve.

- As poverty levels rise in Africa and unemployment becomes a global issue, the need for effective social enterprises is set to increase further.

13
Online Accelerator

As the world around us rapidly shifts, changing the conditions in which every business operates, we all need to adjust, update and modify our patterns of behaviour. In this, our last case study, I'm going to share some of my insights into a programme we started in 2022, namely our online accelerator model. This was in response to the massive and increasing challenge of youth unemployment.

I love this accelerator's scalability and reach, and its potential for further innovation through technology. We had wondered for many years how to translate the inspirational energy generated from our in-person workshops and peer-meetups. Covid changed everything. My family, for example, who were spread across the globe, began to meet every Sunday on Zoom for a chat, connecting more intimately and regularly than we had in our entire lives.

I saw firsthand how this new technology could be a pivotal point for the transformation of existing relationships, which could be easily applied to entire businesses. At Fetola, we eagerly sought ways to use this knowledge in an online accelerator with real potential for scale. This is one of our newest initiatives and remains in the exciting, creative phase.

The future of Africa, and indeed of the world, is in the youth. This accelerator is ideally suited to young entrepreneurs and solutions that optimise their potential, which really excites me.

Overview of the Youth Start-Up Accelerator

The Youth Start-Up Accelerator was developed as a response to the enormous problem of youth unemployment. Its purpose is to help hundreds of promising young entrepreneurs build successful small businesses that survive and grow.

Built for scale and impact, the accelerator balances the need to reach high numbers whilst delivering measurable business success. The Youth Start-Up Accelerator has an annual intake of 100 youth candidates from across the country, at ideation or early start-up stage.

The fully funded, year-long accelerator uses a modified Fetola method to build scale and impact at appropriate cost per entrepreneur.

The accelerator is in two parts:

1. The first six months focuses on identifying and assessing the viability of the candidate's business concept.

2. The second six months analyses the market potential and revenue model. The strongest entrepreneurs are assisted to refine their business models, generate revenue and consolidate their business for further success. Growth support takes the form of interactive online webinars, self-managed accountability groups, open peer groups and mentorship, all of which are designed to ensure a high degree of engagement. Additional one-on-one support is customised to individual needs, for example, in compliance and in pitch preparation for finance applications.

The overall intentions of the accelerator are:

- Rapid transfer of essential business know-how and personal accountability

- The development of an agile growth mindset

Early exposure to the concepts of investment readiness keeps a focus on financial viability and long-term success. A clear growth pathway is provided, supported by practical, applied business skills.

Businesses exit the programme as solid start-ups, with greater self-confidence, a healthy sense of empowerment, and emerging understanding of the essentials of business. Participants who choose to re-enter the job market do so as higher-value employees. Those who stay the distance are better equipped to start and succeed in their own business.

The problems we are addressing

The Youth Start-Up Accelerator seeks to solve a number of challenges:

1. Slow economic growth

South Africa faces persistent, intractable challenges, including rolling blackouts, unstable water supply, and crippling slowdowns in the rail transportation and port systems. Unemployment rates are rising much faster than the economy is growing. This is in contrast with the rest of Africa, which, according to the African Development Bank, is set to outperform the rest of the world in economic growth, with real gross domestic product (GDP) averaging around 4% in 2023 and 2024.[35]

2. Lack of purchasing power

In layman's terms, slow economic growth means that people don't have money to spend. No business can succeed if customers lack the wherewithal to buy their products.

3. Youth unemployment

The supply-side problem this accelerator seeks to address is high, and rising, youth unemployment. According to the International Labour Organization, more than 72 million youth in Africa are not in education, employment or training.[36] In South Africa the youth unemployment rate is especially high, at 50,5% in 2023.[37] Officials estimate that in 2023 there were 4,6 million unemployed youth between the ages of 15 and 35.[38] This means that one in three South Africans of working age are unable to find work.

4. Lack of education

Lack of education and market-related skills amongst the young and their families are linked to crime, the loss of investment, political instability and weak economic growth. It is vital that the type of education provided meets today's needs, especially in the areas of technology and digital skills.

5. Undeveloped business skills

Lack of business experience is a challenge where there is little or no history of entrepreneurship in the family or community. Lack of capital, scarcity thinking, hostility to capitalism, and a dearth of successful role models and mentors are impediments to business formation.

The Why – vision for success

Fetola's vision for the Youth Start-Up Accelerator is to use the internet to increase the number of people starting businesses and improve their success rate. In so doing, we seek to create an expanding ecosystem of thriving small businesses.

The online methodology is most appropriate for youth participants, as most young people are comfortable with and fully embrace technology and online engagement.

In addition, we believe in youth as the future, with Africa set to be the 'youth continent' by 2030.[39] We also know from our own experience in South Africa, and from international studies such as the Global Enterprise Monitor GEM, that successful youth business creation is already happening. As far back as 2011, the estimated 165 million youth entrepreneurs in business globally were reported to generate 12,1 new jobs each, which adds up to a total of more than two billion youth business jobs![40]

The goal of the Youth Start-Up Accelerator is a scalable solution that drives entrepreneurial success efficiently and effectively wherever access to the internet is possible.

What makes it different?

This is an acceleration programme, not a training course. We resist the temptation to reach massive numbers at the expense of quality outcomes, which is an easy trap to fall into when the problem of unemployment is so overwhelming.

Young people often feel deeply frustrated and disappointed after completing training courses that promise to change their lives but leave them unable to experience the personal advancement they anticipated. Fetola's initiative delivers what it promises, empowering the youth who take part in a programme with the skills and resources to turn their inherent entrepreneurial skills into a thriving business.

We do this by focusing on five core actions:

1. Carefully selecting candidates with a genuine and burning desire to become entrepreneurs

2. Providing a simple business road map

3. Continuing interactive engagement, including peer groups and mentoring

4. Teaching applied business skills

5. Providing catalytic start-up grants to leapfrog early growth

In addition, the close partnership with our partners' strategic leadership teams provides young entrepreneurs with access to mentors and role models that would normally be out of their reach. Partners provide training on personal finance, support with investment readiness and personal encouragement, the motivating effect of which can be priceless.

It is these engaging, interactive relationships that are the glue and the inspiration that keep young entrepreneurs engaged and activated. Relationships grow between the entrepreneurs, with the accelerator team, and with stakeholders who care about their success.

Of the 100 aspiring entrepreneurs that started our pilot programme, five dropped out to take up employment or study further. Ninety-five successfully completed phase one, and all of the chosen fifty-three completed phase two. Of these, thirty exited with businesses that were revenue-positive, with potential for further growth. The net promoter score showcasing participant satisfaction levels exceeded 95% across the entire programme.

What can go wrong

Alongside all the positive aspects to the Youth Start-Up Accelerator, there are of course also challenging factors we need to overcome, as detailed below.

1. Candidate selection

There will clearly always be outliers, and the right person with access to resources and skills can start a successful business at any age. However, we know from our own experience and from international data that the ideal age to start a business is around age twenty-eight, once the entrepreneur has gained life experience.[41]

Experience also shows that the ideal candidate is well educated, with a post-matric qualification or higher, and has some working experience. Whilst this does not match the typical demographic of unemployed youth, it matches the candidate with the greatest potential to succeed as an entrepreneur and who can generate jobs for others.

2. Dropout rates

The most obvious danger of online-only accelerator programmes is weak impact caused by high drop-out rates. Online training is notorious for its huge drop-off rates, which globally sit around the 95%

mark.[42] Online learning generally just isn't that inspiring; and when it is provided as a free resource, it's easy and painless to drop without much consequence. Everything the online accelerator does needs to work against these statistics.

3. Poor training content

Training content that is too theoretical, complex or repetitive will not work in an online accelerator. Standard lecture routines with talking heads result in immediate disengagement and low satisfaction scores. It is essential to use applied training methods that are engaging and meaningful to the aspiring entrepreneur. Workshop-style facilitation is needed, with practical insights from experienced entrepreneurs and ongoing discussions in breakaway groups.

4. Reliable, high-speed internet access

Where access to reliable, strong internet is sparse or expensive, this style of online training is difficult, if not impossible. The ability for candidates to listen, watch and engage in the discussions is critical. In these circumstances it's also important that content is delivered in formats that the audience are able to access; material that is data-heavy will not work.

In South Africa data costs are very high, which is why the online accelerator provides a free, monthly data allowance to enable attendance. Sadly, though, during loadshedding, the signal quality in outlying areas is often too weak for online meetings, resulting in poor attendance. Provision of loadshedding devices cannot fix this, so this remains an intractable problem for the accelerator.

5. Engagement

Given the importance of peer-to-peer engagement and peer-to-team engagement, the ability and willingness of participants to access discussion groups on WhatsApp, Signal or other preferred communication channels is fundamental to success. Where this breaks down – for example, because of internet access or interpersonal challenges – disengagement and drop-out results.

6. Mismatched business models

With this low-cost accelerator, it's important to select and guide aspiring entrepreneurs towards business models with a high chance of success. This includes businesses with low barriers to entry that are simple to implement and where there is clear demand. Highly innovative or unproven businesses that have long pathways to success – for example, tech platforms requiring huge financial and time investment – are unsuited to this specific model.

7. Communications

Given the emotional and financial pressure faced by participants desperate for success, and the challenges of online-only engagement, emotions can quickly become derailed if there is a misalignment of expectations. Clear communications from the start, outlining the expectations from both the entrepreneur and the accelerator and repeating these during the onboarding process, are crucial to creating and maintaining trust.

CASE STUDY: Gugu Dladla

Gugulethu Dladla and her sister are great examples of the enthusiasm and potential of young entrepreneurs. As a young female farmer, aged twenty-four, Gugu entered the online Youth Start-Up Accelerator programme as an early-stage entrepreneur with the rudiments of an urban farm.

Urban farming is changing the popular belief that farming is for old people. The Dladla sisters' business, Kusile Bhekilanga Farm, is proof that young, female entrepreneurs can be successful farmers in an urban setting. Located in the North West province of South Africa, the farm produces, packages and sells spinach through a wholly owned farm shop in Tembisa township outside Johannesburg.

Gugu is passionate about contributing positively to the township economy and collaborating with other entrepreneurs in her area. She also holds a marketing management qualification, which is instrumental in helping her drive the business's marketing strategy.

Prior to joining the programme, the Dladla sisters grew spinach in their backyard. As a result of the support they received from the Youth Start-Up Accelerator they have now secured a bigger piece of land, added a new line of washed and cut spinach, and added the farm store as a point of contact.

The programme's catalytic grant funding enabled them to improve their packaging and production systems.

Kusile Bhekilanga Farm experienced a significant revenue growth of 32,43% on the programme – a clear indication that the implementation of the strategies and skills learnt on the accelerator led to improved productivity and profitability. It also highlights the potential for further expansion and impact in the urban farming sector.

Enthusiastic, optimistic, well educated and resilient, Gugulethu was recognised as the most improved entrepreneur on the programme. The sisters left the accelerator more confident in themselves and in their ability to grow their business. They show exciting potential for further growth.

Summary

The emerging success of this online accelerator model has been exciting to watch. It shows good potential as a tool for supporting educated youth with access to the internet, who have self-identified as entrepreneurs and have made practical steps towards their business start-up and early growth.

As online engagement, collaboration and interaction form an essential component of the programme's methodology, it is not suited in this format for those without online access.

It is clear, though, that online acceleration has potential for generating good results in terms of business start-up and early success. As such, it appears to be a viable option in countries such as South Africa, where there is a need to reach thousands of people at appropriately low cost.

As always, selection is critical to success, using tools and methods to identify people with the right entrepreneurial personality, resilience, and commitment to succeed.

When using a modified acceleration model such as this, excitement over the ability to reach large numbers of entrepreneurs needs to be tempered against the resulting reduced depth of impact. Whilst the online acceleration model removes the high expense of individual interaction and, in theory, could be delivered fully self-service and online, the loss of this human engagement and peer interaction is likely to result in low participant engagement, high drop-off and weak impact.

As we continue to refine and advance the online accelerator model, it shows potential for building the size of the start-up pipeline of businesses elsewhere in Africa. If these start-ups are correctly cared for as they enter the pipeline of small businesses, over time this should improve the numbers of quality businesses within the economic ecosystem.

Key takeaways

- Online acceleration supports ideation and early-stage enterprises with a method that is cost-effective and suited to high participation numbers.

- Group mentorship and peer mentoring provides a viable method for the early-stage business and provides opportunities for cross-learning.

- A clear road map to success, and applied, practical skills training are key components to good progress.

- Success factors include the ability to create active two-way engagement amongst peers and between peers and the acceleration team, through the use of interactive webinars, peer groups and check-ins with the support team.

- Challenge factors include difficulties with access to high-speed, cost-effective internet.

- Provision of small amounts of catalytic growth finance has a powerful impact on the early-stage business, especially where access to forms of finance is lacking.

Conclusion

As we come to the end of this book, we can see the beginning of the next chapter of greater reflection on our approach to small business, as a tool for lasting change and deep economic, social and environmental impact.

I have shared with you the essential elements of the Fetola Growth Method and outlined the importance of each element:

- Selection of the right candidates is critical, for without the right leadership the business cannot thrive.

- Mentorship, when done well, provides the support and self-confidence that many entrepreneurs crave.

- Method and planning are vital – just enough to get the right things done, but not so much that it becomes constraining to growth.

- Systems and methods are the foundations of scale, without which the growing business will fall apart.

- Market access and the product–market fit, which so many businesses get wrong, are crucial to success.

- Niche markets, customer diversification, and building a growth ladder towards the more sophisticated and demanding corporate supply chains, are all significant factors.

- Various aspects around money need to be considered, including the emotions around money that hold businesses back.

- Accurate financial records are vital, to inform rational decision making and enable access to growth finance.

- Performance data needs to be collected and reported, providing a critical asset for managing business and accelerator performance, especially for businesses with social and environmental impact.

In Part Two I shared some of the ways these growth methods have been successfully implemented, the problems that each accelerator seeks to address, and a candid section on what can go wrong. Each case study was chosen to give a window into the types of businesses that can be successful, including how and why they succeed.

For many, entrepreneurship remains an enigma – something to be studied at university, and a courageous act that others do as they dream of a better future.

As we have seen, it's all of this and more.

The theory of entrepreneurship is interesting and exciting to read and learn. The practice of being an entrepreneur is different. Starting a business takes courage, and the ability to apply knowledge in a dynamic, ever-changing world. By investing in the successful growth of entrepreneurs, we can significantly increase their chance of success and help them to build a business that lasts. As an entrepreneur who has built and lost businesses myself, I understand the importance of helping people to start, grow and scale businesses that are still in business ten, twenty and even a hundred years later. A solid, sustainable business creates an anchor for the leader, their family, their employees and the families of their employees. More than that, it supports the building of an ecosystem around the business.

The reality is, though, that many billions of rands and dollars are invested by social impact investors, corporate enterprises, supplier development practitioners, development finance institutions and family offices, with little or no lasting effect. We only need to look at the sluggish economy, the high levels of unemployment, and weak local business-to-business ecosystems to see evidence that this money is often spent with little measurable impact.

It's increasingly clear to me just how vital the role of professional acceleration is in ensuring the overall success of impact investing in general, and of social impact investing in particular.

Social impact investing is a form of financing that seeks to create positive change in the world by generating financial returns, and both social and environmental benefits. It is a diverse, growing sector that attracts a range of investors, including foundations, philanthropists, banks, pension funds, corporations and individuals. Investments can include grant, debt, venture capital and equity.

Although small in relation to global impact investing, Africa's nascent impact investment footprint is significant and growing. The Global Impact Investing Network (GIIN) reports of an impact investing market of USD1,164 trillion, with 2% of assets under management in Sub-Saharan Africa.[43] According to their 2020 investor's survey, this is growing at 7% per annum, but only 1% is going to seed start-up phase.[44]

Despite this growing interest, however, the impact investing sector faces four key challenges:

1. Lack of access to sufficient qualified investment pipeline

2. Inability to secure cost-effective deals

3. Frequent post-investment failure

4. Ongoing challenges with effective measurement and reporting

Professional small-business accelerators such as those we have been exploring are ideally positioned to help solve these challenges. They can:

- **Grow a pipeline** of investment ready businesses through professional pre-investment support including acceleration

- **Secure deals** by building SMME investment readiness, de-risking investment and supporting successful negotiations

- **Deliver post-investment support** that increases investment success

- **Align monitoring and evaluation tools and metrics** to ensure high accuracy and consistency of verified data, which is meaningful at enterprise and fund levels

Using acceleration as a tool, professional working partnerships between the impact intermediary and the impact investor increase deal flow. They help to de-risk the investment, which reduces the cost of finance for the enterprise and increases the success rate of investment. This leads to a virtuous cycle of investment success, significantly increasing the resulting social and environmental impact.

I hope this book has shown you – and others like you, who are passionate about improving the future through the development of thriving small businesses – that success is possible when we use the right tools in the right way, with the right entrepreneurs. It is possible when we work together, challenging each other, supporting each other and constantly asking the questions:

Is this the best way to spend this money?

What is the return on investment?

This book has given you a snapshot of Fetola's current growth methods and some of the accelerators we have implemented, but the job is not done. To help entrepreneurs succeed, we have to stay one step ahead in their rapidly changing world.

This requires ongoing innovation, new technology solutions, new ways to build thriving ecosystems, and new investment methods and partners. At Fetola we are excited about our critical success role with social impact investors and our catalytic investment tools. We are finding ways to invest in small businesses when they really need it, which is long before the traditional investors are interested, and beyond the scope of micro loans. We are also committed to our work as drivers of circular economy practices through the small-business ecosystem, so that these practices become the norm.

Building a thriving small-business ecosystem sometimes seems like building an ever-changing jigsaw puzzle. The pieces keep moving and growing, and sometimes disappearing, but the obsessive drive of the true entrepreneur compels us to persist until finally, hopefully, the puzzle is complete.

Our job as accelerators is to identify those driven personalities with the passion and purpose to embark on a journey, to invest in their dreams, to walk alongside them, to encourage and guide them – all without trying to take over – as they launch into the world and take flight to make their own impact.

Our job as professional social impact intermediaries is to use these skills to ensure the virtuous cycle of social impact investing success, thereby catalysing lasting results.

Every day I ask myself the questions:

Are we investing our time and resources in the right businesses and in the right way, and what can we learn and do better?

Are we partnering with the right people to scale this success so that together we can build a billion better lives across the globe?

If you are considering the same questions and would like to improve your own social and economic impact, by either investing directly into scalable initiatives or supporting others to do so, why not complete the Big Opportunities in Small Business Heat Map at www. fetola.co.za/heatmap and reach out to get connected?

We are not done yet – let's find ways to work together!

What Next?

If you've enjoyed this book and would like to learn more about working with Fetola to unlock big opportunities in small business, you can:

- Complete your Big Opportunities in Small Business Heat Map at www.fetola.co.za/heatmap

- Visit www.fetola.co.za/bookasession to book a Big Opportunities in Small Business strategy session

- See our list of upcoming events at www.fetola. co.za/events and attend one of our workshops

Notes

1   Productivity SA, 'Our 2030 goal: 1 million jobs created by SMMEs in South Africa' (6 June 2022), https://productivitysa.co.za/productivitysa.co.za/blog/our-2030-goal-1-million-jobs-created-by-smmes-in-south-africa/index.html, accessed 28 June 2024

2   International Association of Event Hosts, 'Environmental impacts' (no date), www.eventhosts.org/resources/event-impact-standards/environmental-impacts-2, accessed 18 April 2024

3   I Valodia, 'South Africa can't crack the inequality curse: Why, and what can be done', *The Conversation* (14 September 2023), https://theconversation.com/south-africa-cant-crack-the-inequality-curse-why-and-what-can-be-done-213132, accessed 25 January 2024

4   A O'Neill, 'South Africa: Youth unemployment rate from 2004 to 2023', Statista (8 April 2024), www.statista.com/statistics/813010/youth-unemployment-rate-in-south-africa, accessed 18 April 2024

5   National Planning Commission of South Africa, *National Development Plan – 2030* (NPC, 2012), 'Chapter Three: Economy and employment', www.nationalplanningcommission.org.za/assets/Documents/NDP_Chapters/NDP%20 2030-CH3-Economy%20and%20employment.pdf, accessed 18 April 2024

6   S Chamine, PQ® Training, www.positiveintelligence.com/program, accessed 21 April 2024

7   JF Demartini, *The Breakthrough Experience: A revolutionary new approach to personal transformation* (Hay House UK, 2009)

8   University of the Witwatersrand Johannesburg, 'Mental health in SA is at shocking levels but people are not seeking help', *Wits University Research News* (14 November 2022), www.wits.ac.za/news/latest-news/research-news/2022/2022-11/mental-health-in-sa-is-at-shocking-levels-but-people-are-not-seeking-help-.html, accessed 28 June 2024

9   R Branson, 'Screw it, let's do it', Virgin (April 2006), www.virgin.com/branson-family/books/richard-branson/screw-it-lets-do-it, accessed 24 April 2024

10   C Howe, 'Simply making a difference', ec@ps
      (no date), www.ecaps.co/wp-content/uploads/
      ec@ps-outline.pdf, accessed 21 April 2024

11   N Maseko, *Welcome to Financial Freedom: Get in the
      game and play to win* (Digital on Demand, 2022)

12   Outlier Reporter, '83% matric pass rate, but is
      SA making the grade?', *The Outlier* (19 January
      2024), www.theoutlier.co.za/education/2024-01-
      19/86739/2023-matric-results, accessed 28 June
      2024

13   Department of Trade, Industry and Competition,
      Broad-Based Black Economic Empowerment,
      2013 (Act No. 46 of 2013), Republic of South
      Africa (24 October 2014), www.thedtic.gov.za/
      financial-and-non-financial-support/b-bbee/
      broad-based-black-economic-empowerment,
      accessed 27 April 2024

14   UNCTAD, 'Total and urban population',
      UNCTAD Handbook of Statistics 2023 (2023),
      https://hbs.unctad.org/total-and-urban-
      population, accessed 24 April 2024

15   C Wijnberg, 'Your Rand is worth more than you
      think', *IOL* (17 August 2020), www.iol.co.za/
      opinion/your-rand-is-worth-more-than-you-
      think-07fa0dee-3997-5a82-9217-039807aff139,
      accessed 25 April 2024

16   N Cowling, 'Population that received social
      grants, relief assistance or social relief in South
      Africa in 2019, by province', Statista (26 April
      2023), www.statista.com/statistics/1116081/
      population-receiving-social-grants-in-south-
      africa-by-province, accessed 25 April 2024

17 Small Enterprise Development Agency, *SMME Quarterly Update, 3rd Quarter 2022* (SEDA, 2023), www.seda.org.za/Publications/Pages/Research-Publications.aspx, accessed 25 April 2024

18 SAB Foundation, *SAB Foundation Tholoana Enterprise Programme Impact Report – January 2015 to March 2022* (2023), https://fetola.co.za/wp-content/uploads/2023/03/TholoanaEnterpriseProgramme-ImpactReport202381.pdf, accessed 28 June 2024

19 M Dodd, *The Man Who Stopped the Desert* (1080 Films, 2010), www.amazon.com/Man-Who-Stopped-Desert/dp/B078J6RZFM, accessed 25 April 2024

20 BizCommunity, '11% of South Africans still live in squatter shacks' (17 September 2007), www.bizcommunity.com/Article/196/19/18108.html, accessed 25 April 2024

21 Rogerwilco and Survey54, *The 2023 Township CX Report* (Rogerwilco and Survey54, 2023), www.rogerwilco.co.za/sites/default/files/2023-06/Township-CX-Report-2023.pdf, accessed 23 July 2024

22 Z Dyomfana, 'Black tax – burden or investment?', Investec (28 April 2022), www.investec.com/en_za/focus/investing/black-tax.html, accessed 25 April 2024

23 A Charman, L Petersen and T Govender, *Township Economy: People, spaces and practices* (HSRC Press, 2020)

24 World Meteorological Organization, *WMO Atlas of Mortality and Economic Losses from Weather, Climate and Water Extremes (1970–2019)* (WMO, 2021), https://library.wmo.int/idurl/4/57564, accessed 26 April 2024

25 Transparency International, 'Corruption Perceptions Index 2021' (2021), www.transparency.org/en/cpi/2021, accessed 26 April 2024

26 L Godfrey, 'The circular economy as development opportunity', Council of Scientific & Industrial Research (2021), www.circulareconomy.co.za/wp-content/uploads/2021/12/CSIR-2021-Circular-Economy-As-Development-Opportunity.pdf, accessed 26 April 2024

27 Ellen MacArthur Foundation, www.ellenmacarthurfoundation.org, accessed 26 April 2024

28 A Grant, *Think Again* (Viking Books, 2021)

29 Trading Economics, 'South Africa unemployment rate' (2024), https://tradingeconomics.com/south-africa/unemployment-rate, accessed 29 August 2024

30 S Sinek, 'Episode 106: The value of values, with Walmart CEO Doug McMillon', *A Bit Of Optimism* [podcast] (5 December 2023), https://simonsinek.com/podcast/episodes/the-value-of-values-with-walmart-ceo-doug-mcmillon, accessed 27 April 2024

31 United Nations Development Programme, 'What are the Sustainable Development Goals?', www.undp.org/sustainable-development-goals, accessed 27 April 2024

32 JobsNowAfrica, www.jobsnowafrica.org/about/charter, accessed 27 April 2024

33 Outlier Reporter, '83% matric pass rate, but is SA making the grade?', *The Outlier* (19 January 2024), www.theoutlier.co.za/education/2024-01-19/86739/2023-matric-results, accessed 28 June 2024

34 UN Women, 'Facts and figures: Ending violence against women' (21 September 2023), www.unwomen.org/en/what-we-do/ending-violence-against-women/facts-and-figures, accessed 27 April 2024

35 African Development Bank Group, 'Africa's economic growth to outpace global forecast in 2023-2024 – African Development Bank biannual report' (19 January 2023), www.afdb.org/en/news-and-events/press-releases/africas-economic-growth-outpace-global-forecast-2023-2024-african-development-bank-biannual-report-58293, accessed 27 April 2023

36 International Labour Organization, 'African youth face pressing challenges in the transition from school to work', ILOSTAT (10 August 2023), https://ilostat.ilo.org/blog/african-youth-face-pressing-challenges-in-the-transition-from-school-to-work, accessed 27 April 2024

37　A O'Neill, 'South Africa: Youth unemployment rate from 2004 to 2023', Statista (8 April 2024), www.statista.com/statistics/813010/youth-unemployment-rate-in-south-africa, accessed 18 April 2024

38　South African Government, 'Statistics South Africa on quarterly Labour Force Survey quarter three 2023', www.gov.za/news/media-statements/statistics-south-africa-quarterly-labour-force-survey-quarter-three-2023-14, accessed 27 April 2024

39　C Vogel and G Ziervogel, 'Climate change impacts in Africa and the role of urbanization and youth', *Our Warming Planet* (November 2021), www.worldscientific.com/doi/abs/10.1142/9789811238222_0017, accessed 28 April 2024

40　DJ Kelley et al, *Global Entrepreneurship Monitor: 2011 global report* (GEM, 2015), www.gemconsortium.org/file/open?fileId=48371, accessed 27 April 2024

41　T Ryan, 'What's the ideal age to start a retail business?', *RetailWire* (10 September 2021), https://retailwire.com/discussion/whats-the-ideal-age-to-start-a-retail-business, accessed 28 April 2024

42　Jessica, 'Are your e-learning course dropout rates costing your business?', Obrizum (26 September 2023), https://obrizum.com/resources/are-your-e-learning-course-dropout-rates-costing-your-business, accessed 28 April 2024

43 D Hand, B Ringel and A Danel, *GIINsight: Sizing the Impact Investing Market 2022* (GIIN, 2022), https://thegiin.org/publication/research/impact-investing-market-size-2022, accessed 29 August 2024

44 D Hand, B Ringel and A Danel, *GIINsight: Sizing the Impact Investing Market 2022* (GIIN, 2022), https://thegiin.org/publication/research/impact-investing-market-size-2022, accessed 29 August 2024

45 C Wijnberg, *Sheep Will Never Rule the World* (Quivertree Publications, April 2020)

Acknowledgements

No success is an individual journey, and I would not have been able to create a company that delivers so much positive impact if it weren't for the people who work alongside me, supporting me and passionately applying their energies to this task.

I would specifically like to acknowledge the contribution of Anton Ressel, who has walked this journey since the very beginning. His wisdom and talent, as a Fetola trainer, costing and pricing guru and award-winning mentor, have been of great support. Similarly, I want to thank Chantal Terry, who joined me in the very early days of Fetola and has grown as the business has grown. She has provided her own calm insights, people skills and personal passion for making a lasting difference, especially to the women of South Africa, and to those living in the small towns and villages across the country. Chantal's personal journey of self-discovery and empowerment has brought a rich value to those she touches.

Terrena Rathanlall's careful editing and writing support has helped to turn this into a book of note.

My young team of bright minds includes Grant Prince, who stood out from his first few weeks as an intern willing to go the extra mile and who has risen through the ranks to play a significant leadership role. Isabel du Toit, who joined as an intern in need of close guidance and has become our go-to person for efficiency and method. The circular economy specialist in the team, Busi Bebeza, emerged to become an exceptional programme manager and passionate developer of youth talent.

I want to acknowledge all the people that have gravitated to Fetola – mentors, trainers, interns from across the world, administrators, creatives and board members – each one bringing a gift and adding a brick in the wall of success.

Thanks to our clients, who believed in us, invested with us and trusted us to do our best, co-creating lasting impact and a positive difference that will be felt for generations. To the thousands of entrepreneurs who have graced our doors and walked their journey of growth with us – entrepreneurs with the courage to start and grow their business, and the humility to reach out and ask for help along the journey. Your success is our success, and I thank you for it.

This book is also dedicated to all the people that have challenged me in life. It is this concept of learning through challenge that underpins the ethos of Fetola – it is only when we engage in struggle that we really learn. That is why true entrepreneurship is not simply a set of theories we can learn, but also a journey that we experience. It's a journey we emerge from wiser, stronger and more successful.

Lastly, I would like to tip my hat at genetics and acknowledge my maternal English grandmother, who was a marvel ahead of her time, and who believed in me and fought for my individuality; and to my paternal South African/Scottish grandmother, who taught me the lessons of fortitude and hard work.

The Author

Catherine Wijnberg is a seasoned business leader and serial entrepreneur. She is a visionary, dedicated to leveraging small businesses as agents of empowerment, inclusive economic growth, social wellbeing and job creation. With a profound belief in the transformative power of collaboration, Catherine envisions catalysing change at an ecosystem level, impacting millions of lives. She embodies the spirit of entrepreneurship, leadership, and unwavering commitment to making a meaningful difference in the world.

As the group CEO and founder of Fetola, Catherine leads a dynamic team of growth professionals committed to nurturing businesses. Through Fetola, she has spearheaded initiatives that have fostered thousands of reliable, responsible and resilient businesses, serving as the bedrock of local economies and stimulating positive change in communities across South Africa. Her dream for Fetola extends beyond mere business success. She envisions Fetola as a haven, where talented individuals unleash their full potential to collectively weave magic into the world by facilitating the success of others.

Fetola's business accelerators under Catherine's leadership cater to a diverse array of enterprises, including emerging rural and peri-urban businesses, circular economy initiatives, social enterprises, and youth start-ups, across various sectors, spanning agriculture, alternative energy, health care, manufacturing and more.

Born in Zambia and educated across England, Scotland and Australia, Catherine holds a master's degree in agriculture from the University of Queensland, Australia and an MBA from Henley Business School, UK. Her expertise in personal development, leadership and business growth has been instrumental in launching multiple ventures across southern Africa, ranging from agriculture and transportation to hospitality.

Catherine's impact transcends the boardroom. Her much-loved book, *Sheep Will Never Rule the World*, offers invaluable insights into personal and business growth, inspiring readers from C-suite executives to aspiring young entrepreneurs.[45]

Beyond her professional pursuits, Catherine finds joy in the simple pleasures of life. A mother of three girls, she resides in Cape Town, where she indulges her passions for paragliding, running, mountain hiking, artistry, birding and wildlife conservation.

⊕ www.catherinewijnberg.com

▦ www.linkedin.com/in/catherine-wijnberg-5142049

www.ingramcontent.com/pod-product-compliance
Lightning Source LLC
Chambersburg PA
CBHW071542200326
41519CB00021BB/6579